Finland-Swedes in Michigan

T0158350

DISCOVERING THE PEOPLES OF MICHIGAN

Arthur W. Helweg, Russell M. Magnaghi, and Linwood H. Cousins, *Series Editors*

Ethnicity in Michigan: Issues and People
Jack Glazier and Arthur W. Helweg

Discovering the Peoples of Michigan is a series of publications examining the state's rich multicultural heritage. The series makes available an interesting, affordable, and varied collection of books that enables students and educated lay readers to explore Michigan's ethnic dynamics. A knowledge of the state's rapidly changing multicultural history has far-reaching implications for human relations, education, public policy, and planning. We believe that Discovering the Peoples of Michigan will enhance understanding of the unique contributions that diverse and often unrecognized communities have made to Michigan's history and culture.

Finland-Swedes in Michigan

Mika Roinila

Michigan State University Press

East Lansing

⊚ The paper used in this publication meets the minimum requirements
of ANSI/NISO Z39.48-1992 (R 1997) (Permanence of Paper).

Michigan State University Press
East Lansing, Michigan 48823-5245

Printed and bound in the United States of America.

19 18 17 16 15 14 13 12   1 2 3 4 5 6 7 8 9 10

LIBRARY OF CONGRESS CATALOGING-IN-PUBLICATION DATA
Roinila, Mika.
Finland-Swedes in Michigan / Mika Roinila.
p. cm.
Includes bibliographical references and index.
ISBN 978-1-61186-030-6 (pbk. : alk. paper) 1. Finland-Swedes—Michigan—History.
2. Finland-Swedes—Michigan—Social conditions. 3. Finnish Americans—Michigan—History.
4. Finnish Americans—Michigan—Social conditions. 5. Finns—Michigan—History.
6. Michigan—Ethnic relations—History. 7. Finland—Emigration and immigration—History.
8. Michigan—Emigration and immigration—History. I. Title.
F575.F5R65 2012
977.4'0049454—dc23
2011027336

Cover design by Ariana Grabec-Dingman
Book design by Charlie Sharp, Sharp Des!gns, Lansing, Michigan

Cover photograph of John and Charles Strandholm, commercial fishing with nets
on Lake Superior at Hessel, 1900 taken by the author from John A. Markstrom file
in Myhrman Collection, Abo Akademi, Åbo (Turku), Finland, 2010.

Michigan State University Press is a member of the Green Press Initiative and
is committed to developing and encouraging ecologically responsible publishing practices. For more information about the Green Press Initiative and the use
of recycled paper in book publishing, please visit *www.greenpressinitiative.org*.

Visit Michigan State University Press at *www.msupress.msu.edu*

ACKNOWLEDGMENTS

Numerous people have helped in the compilation of this work. Without their assistance, the insights and understanding of the Finland-Swedes in Michigan would be sadly lacking. Credit goes to graduate student Anders Gillis, who began this project with the supervision of Dr. Russell M. Magnaghi at Northern Michigan University. Their interest in Finland-Swedes was the impetus for this manuscript. I would also like to thank Shelley Blochert of Ludington, Rev. Scott Harmon of Escanaba, and the many current and former Michigan residents I have spoken to or contacted over the past year. Thanks to Syrene Forsman and the Swedish-Finn Historical Society in Seattle for your valuable help and support with this project. Thanks also to Jason Glatz of Western Michigan University for his excellent cartographic work. Special thanks go to Dr. Arnold Alanen of the University of Wisconsin for his continued support, guidance, and encouragement in my quest to collect historic census data that now sees the light of day. I would especially like to thank Bethel College graduate students Kristen Hopewell, Allison Marsh, and Theresa Phelps for the many hours of painstaking census work they spent in tabulating Swedish-speaking Finns in Wayne County found in the 1930 census data. Finally, thanks go to Finlandia Foundation National for their financial support of this undertaking. Any errors in this manuscript are solely mine.

Contents

Introduction

The Finland-Swedes are pre-Viking descendants who settled on the Åland Islands and the coastal margins of today's Southern and Western Finland. They lived in Finland prior to the 1200s and were part of the Kingdom of Sweden until 1809. For the many thousands of Finland-Swede emigrants who found their way to North America in the late 1800s and the early 1900s, the term "Finland-Swede" may not accurately identify the people described in this book. Today defined as natives of Finland with a Swedish mother tongue, this immigrant population involves many who left the Grand Duchy of Finland during the reign of Russian czars between 1809 and 1917 and immigrated to North America with different identities. The majority of the population in the Grand Duchy during this period was Finnish speaking, while a minority of people in the coastal margins spoke Swedish. The Russification of Finland after the turn of the century pushed for the assimilation of Russian language, which in turn alienated many Finnish and Swedish-speaking Finns. These early immigrants identified themselves at times as Russian Swedes, Swede Finns, or simply Swedes. Others have also identified themselves as Ålanders. Whatever term is preferred, this book examines the Finland-Swedes of Michigan and tries to shed light on a small ethnolinguistic minority that few are familiar with.

Immigration to the United States

Similar to other ethnic groups who found North America to their liking, several waves of emigration affected Finland. The first major wave occurred between 1864 and 1913. The first Finnish emigrants to head to North America began from northern Norway in 1864, destined for the agricultural regions of Minnesota and the mines of Michigan's Upper Peninsula. Prior to 1887, only 21,000 had arrived from Finland.[1] Between 1887 and 1892, some 40,000 immigrants arrived.[2] The strongest overseas emigration during the first wave occurred between 1893 and 1913, when over 260,000 Finns left the country, with most settling in the United States.[3] Of this number, over 40,000 came from Swedish-speaking rural parishes in Finland (see map 1).[4] The large influx of all immigrants was curtailed by the restrictive American quota laws passed in 1921 and 1924. In 1924 only 471 immigrants from Finland were allowed into the United States, while a year earlier some 12,000 were admitted.[5] Still, this was the period of a second major wave of emigration from Finland that took place after World War I. Between 1920 and 1929, some 55,000 immigrants arrived in North America, but due to the changes in immigration laws, most settled in Canada.

Up to 1930 some 400,000 emigrants left for North America. Of this total, some 320,000 settled in the United States, and 80,000 in Canada. Some have estimated that a third of all immigrants returned to Finland for good. Some scholars have calculated that by 1930 Finland-Swedes and their descendants accounted for 80,000–85,000 individuals, or about 20 percent of the total immigrant population on the continent, while others dispute these figures.[6] Allowing for return migration and also for the deaths among Finland-Swedes for the whole period, there may have been about 35,000 of these immigrants in the United States and Canada in 1930.[7]

Identifying the number of Finland-Swedes in the United States has always been very difficult or impossible, because available census statistics simply do not isolate the mother tongue from the country of birth. Until recently, the only method of establishing numbers has been the painstaking, manual analysis of the original manuscripts tabulated by census enumerators. In the past, the way to get to such data—thousands of pages and millions of entries—was through microfilmed versions of the original manuscripts, which are available in libraries and state historical societies. Today, census tabulations are available online for anyone interested in researching material from the 1800s to 1930. Among the best-known online sources are Ancestry.com and HeritageQuest Online.[8] Material obtained through these sources provides 100 percent coverage of all individuals encountered in the country, and, depending on the census year involved, it also provides various details on birthplace, age, marital status, ethnic ancestry, language spoken, occupation, and so on. In order to identify Finland-Swedes, it is possible to see birthplace (Finland) and language spoken (Swedish), which helps identify the number of Finland-Swedes who arrived from Finland. Of all the census years, the 1930 census provides the best data in identifying the number of Finland-Swedes in the country and in Michigan.

However, a sampling of these census data is available today through Integrated Public Use Microdata Series (IPUMS) at the Minnesota Population Center. Through this source, it is possible to discover some of the complexities of linguistic abilities and the trends in the use of languages in the homes of all ethnic groups in the United States, including the Finland-Swedes.[9] Unfortunately, a major restriction is that IPUMS uses a small data sample. The IPUMS-USA uses a 1 percent sample through a 1-in-100 national random sample of the population for the 1910–1970 census periods, while a 5 percent sample, or a 1-in-20 national random sample, of the population is used for 1980–2000 census counts. For this book, I will use data available from both

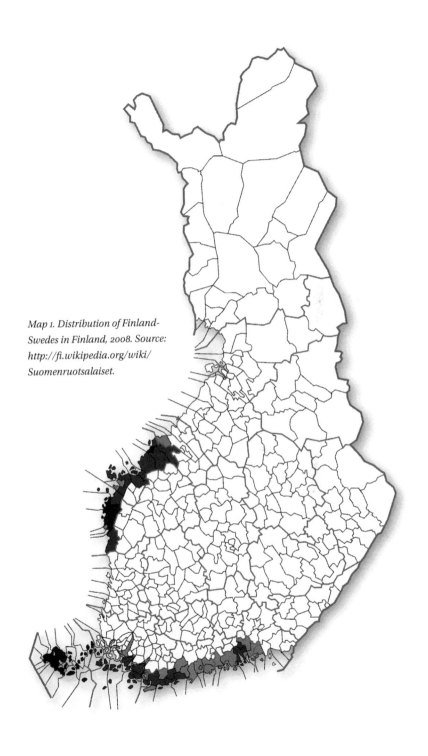

Map 1. Distribution of Finland-Swedes in Finland, 2008. Source: http://fi.wikipedia.org/wiki/Suomenruotsalaiset.

the detailed manuscript records as well as the IPUMS-USA sources, hoping that the two methods will support each other in their findings.

Because of the above data source, the total number of Finland-Swedes (born in Finland with Swedish mother tongue/language) in the United States, along with the proportion of Finland-Swedes among the total Finland born population of the country for each census year can be determined. According to IPUMS-USA, the highest number of Finland-Swedes in the United States was reached in the 1920 census, when nearly 20,000 were identified.[10] For the 1930 census, there were nearly 18,000 Finland-Swedes in the country.

These numbers represent only the members within a household that were born in Finland. Children born in America were not included. Additional descendants in successive generations who may have lost their identity and/or language may be impossible to determine through statistics as well. Overall, a rather steady decline in the number of Finland-Swedes within the country is evident, and in the 2000 census, the Finland-Swedes represented only 6 percent of the total Finnish immigrant population in the country (table 1).

As there is no way to validate the accuracy of census data through detailed examinations of any census counts after 1930, the most recent census that is available for manuscript analysis is the 1930 census available through online sources, as noted earlier. Since the census manuscripts are currently available only through 1930, I hand-counted the data for that year. The results presented here offer the first detailed analysis of Finland-Swedes in any state where large numbers of these immigrants settled.

Reasons for Emigrating

Many reasons for a disproportionate number of Finland-Swedish emigrants from Finland have been proposed by scholars. Economic reasons have been cited as the greatest cause for emigration, but the process of Russification and the obligation to do military service were also big reasons.[11] "My father's cousin, Anders Sandbacka, was removed from his ministerial studies at Uppsala [University] and sent to America because of the imminent danger of being drafted into the Russian Army. He resumed his studies at Augustana College."[12]

Some have argued that Finland-Swedes had a more restless disposition than the Finns. Due to their association with the sea, shipping, fishing, and

Table 1. Finland-Swedes in the United States, 1910–2000 as Estimated by IPUMS-USA

	1910	1920	1930	1940	1960	1980	1990	2000
Total born in Finland								
	126,105	148,058	143,218	113,694	64,446	30,240	23,035	23,199
Total Finland-Swedes								
	16,135	19,789	17,776	13,300	10,755	2,620	1,647	1,402
Percentage Finland-Swedes								
	12.8	13.4	12.4	11.7	16.7	8.7	7.1	6.0

Note: 1940 data used the Sample Line Weight (SLWT), which is defined as the number of persons in the general population represented by each sample-line person in 1940. For all other census years, the IPUMS samples are unweighted "flat" samples using the Person Weight (PERWT), which indicates how many persons in the U.S. population are represented by a given person in an IPUMS sample.
Source: Author tabulation using *http://usa.ipums.org/usa/*.

trade with Sweden, they were seen as a mobile people more willing to migrate than the Finns, who lived predominantly in the interior and were not as easily moved. The Finnish lifestyle involved an immobile, agricultural society.[13] Political opinions, social pressures, and religious bigotry also played a role.[14] Finally, with the transfer of Finland to Russia in 1809, the Ostrobothnian region, which once was centrally located as part of the union of Sweden-Finland, became increasingly peripheral to the influence of the Russian capital of St. Petersburg, which opened the opportunity for emigration.[15]

For whatever reason Finland-Swedes left their homeland, these early immigrants had several options for identifying themselves. They could call themselves Russians (an unlikely scenario, but possible due to political correctness), Russian Swedes, or Swedes. Some identified themselves as Finns, but because of the difficulties involved with communicating in the Finnish and Swedish languages, many of the early attempts at joint organizations with Finnish and Swedish-speaking Finns were discontinued, leading to association with Swedish-speaking immigrants and/or Finnish-speaking immigrants only.[16]

Many identified themselves as Swedes simply because of the similarities in language that they shared with Sweden, which caused confusion when third-generation descendants could not determine their true origins. As noted by a Finland-Swede resident in Baltimore, "many Swedish Finns who came to America before 1900 . . . insisted on calling themselves Swedes instead of Finns. It was not until much after, after currents of nationalism swept Finland that Swedish Finns began to identify themselves as Finns."[17]

With the independence of Finland in 1917 and the aftermath of the Finnish Civil War, "Finland-Swede" (*Finlandssvenska* in Swedish; *Suomenruotsalainen* in Finnish) was the officially recognized term for the Finnish-Swedish ethnolinguistic minority in 1919.

However, the use of the term "Swede-Finn" became a dominant term among the earlier immigrants, and this identity has remained intact to the present. Among later arrivals, the term "Finland-Swede" is more commonly used, and there are still others who identify themselves simply as Swedish or Finnish. In the end, the Finland-Swedish community is a difficult group to investigate due to the myriad ways in which its members can be identified.

Settlement in America

In the 1500s, 1600s, and 1700s, many Finland-Swedes worked in Swedish copper and iron mines in the winter months and returned to Finland during the summer.[18] Between 1790 and 1867, many Finland-Swedes worked as sailors, shipwrights, seamen, skippers, clergy, and company officials with the Russian America Company, which took Finland-Swedes to Alaska. Emigration from Finland was also often forced, and many fled to Sweden as a result of the Great Northern War in the 1700s and the 1809 Russian takeover of Finland.[19]

Some Finland-Swedes made their way to California after the discovery of gold in 1848, while sailors abandoned their ships in order to find a new life. The Crimean War (1854-1855) resulted in the sale of many Finnish ships that were docked in American ports. The result was the desertion of several hundred sailors.[20] By the beginning of the 1860s, there were very likely several hundred sailors from Finland living in America, many of whom later returned to Finland and spread the news about America to their countrymen.[21] Large-scale Finland-Swedish emigration to America began from the southern Ostrobothnian communities in the early 1870s.

The majority of immigrants who arrived in America prior to 1900 originated from the rural areas of Finland and included cottagers, farmers, and crofters, who made up as many as 70 percent of all immigrants. Craftsmen

Pehr Kalm

Pehr Kalm (b. in Sweden 6 Mar 1716; d. in Finland 16 Nov 1779) was educated in Finland and Sweden. He met the leading European naturalist, Linnaeus, in 1741, and under his influence became an expert on botanical applications to agriculture. Linnaeus proposed a trip to North America to discover plants that might be viable in Scandinavia and chose Kalm, who reached Philadelphia in September 1748, to meet the foremost American naturalists. Arriving in New France in July 1749, he botanized near Lake Champlain before moving on to Montréal and Québec. His work there was financed by the French as a favour to Sweden. He met the leading scientific lights, including Jean-François Gaultier and Governor La Galissonière. He returned to New York that autumn but made a botanical foray to Niagara during the summer of 1750. Returning to Sweden in 1751, he took up a professorship at Åbo. Kalm's record of his visit to New France, published 1753–61, offers one of the best studies of intellectual and social life during the final years of the French regime. Besides providing new botanical information, it brought Canada to European attention. In his diary he stated that the scientific interest exhibited by the French was superior to that of the British Americans.

Source: Richard A. Jarrell, "Pehr Kalm," in *The Canadian Encyclopedia*, available at http://www.thecanadianencyclopedia.com/index.cfm?PgNm=TCE&Params=A1ARTA0004214 (Accessed January 7, 2011).

and workers made up some 16 percent of all emigrants, and only 14 percent included other occupations, such as businessmen, entrepreneurs, and educated individuals.[22] The pattern of settlement across the United States had become discernible by 1900 (see map 2). The first of several concentrations was found in the eastern states. Finland-Swedes settled mostly in New York, where the majority of the men were engaged in the building trades, others in factory work. Finland-Swedes also settled in large numbers in Massachusetts, most notably in Worcester, where many were engaged in metal manufacturing, and in Gardner, where furniture manufacturing was a dominant occupation. There were also smaller settlements in Boston, Quincy, Norwood, Springfield, and Fitchburg, along with Woonsocket, Rhode Island.[23] There was also for a time a considerable settlement of Finland-Swedes in Philadelphia, and their influence was noted in the 1926 construction of the John

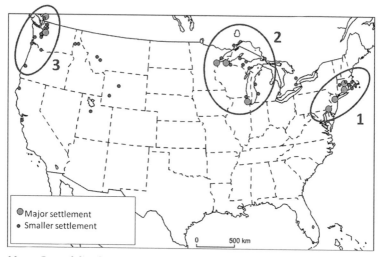

Map 2. *General distribution of Finland-Swedes in North America, early 1900s. Source: Adapted from Mika Roinila, "Finland-Swedish Experience in North America," Journal of Finnish Studies 13, no. 1 (2009): 58–66.*

Hanson–John Morton Memorial Building that eventually became known as the American Swedish Historical Museum. The museum maintains two exhibition rooms named after famous Finland-Swedes, the botanist Pehr Kalm (1716–1779) and women's rights activist Fredrika Bremer (1801–1865).[24]

A second major concentration of Finland-Swedes was found in the Midwest, in a broad area including lower and upper Michigan, Wisconsin, Minnesota, and northern Illinois. In the early period, most of the newcomers found their economic opportunities in the lumber and mining industries, with smaller numbers in manufacturing and the building trades. In many places farming and fishing became the chief occupation. Chicago and Waukegan, Illinois; Duluth and the mining towns on the Mesabi Range in Minnesota; and Superior and Ashland, Wisconsin, were home to many Swedish immigrants from Finland at the turn of the century.[25]

The West Coast established itself as a third concentration of Finland-Swedes. The Pacific Northwest has remained the most important concentration for Finland-Swedes, particularly Seattle, as well as Tacoma, Everett, Olympia, Mount Vernon, Rochester, Aberdeen, and Hoquiam in Washington; Portland, Astoria, and the Coos Bay region in Oregon; and Eureka and the San Francisco Bay area in California. The early occupations in these locations also included lumbering, farming, fishing, and the building trades.[26] While the mining industry attracted many to the mountain states to work in mines located in Leadville and Telluride, Colorado; Butte and Anaconda, Montana; Eureka and Bingham Canyon, Utah; along with Kellogg and Wallace, Idaho, most of these Finland-Swedes later moved to the West Coast.[27]

In estimating the number of Finland-Swedes across the country, IPUMS-USA provides a good start to understanding the distribution by state (see table 2). While Finland-Swedes appear to be present in several states through all census periods, there are irregularities as some states show the presence and/or the absence of Finland-Swedes over time. For example, why would Minnesota have no Finland-Swedes in the 2000 census while in other years they were represented, especially when Minnesota has always had one of the largest populations in the nation? Why does the number of Finland-Swedes drop drastically from 1920 to 1930 in states such as Michigan, Massachusetts, and Minnesota? It is also suspicious that the 1940 numbers appear to be rounded off compared to other census years. Aside from the use of a small sample to establish these numbers, there may be other reasons that explain such statistical variance, such as a 1 percent or 5 percent tabulation of manuscript data, use of weighted samples that vary between years, statistical models and equations that provide overall results, and incorrect reporting by respondents. These are some of the problems encountered with data that does not include everyone. Too many questions are left without answers, and thus a more complete analysis of available information is needed.

For detailed and complex studies, researchers can access information through a Research Data Center (RDC) established by the Center for Economic Studies (CES) of the U.S. Bureau of the Census. There are twelve locations across the country in which RDCs are located, including the University of Michigan, which allows for researchers to study nonpublic microdata collected by the Census Bureau. These microdata files contain data that cannot be released publicly because they contain detailed information on geographic location and/or other characteristics about households that could disclose their identities. The required application process to gain access is long and sometimes difficult, and researchers planning to use an RDC must submit a research proposal, which is reviewed by numerous federal agencies.[28]

Table 2. Top States with Finland-Swedes in the United States, According to 1910-2000 Census Information as Estimated by IPUMS-USA

	Born in Finland with Swedish mother tongue					Born in Finland with Swedish spoken at home		
	1910	1920	1930	1940	1960	1980	1990	2000
California	1,605	1,817	1,818	800	1,490	480	382	334
Connecticut	600	909	909	400	300	180	132	118
Illinois	600	505	707	500	498	40	48	
Massachusetts	602	1,816	2,323	1,200	498	140	75	46
Michigan	2,905	3,232	2,525	1,100	399	80	53	82
Minnesota	1,204	2,197	598	700	996	100	74	
New Jersey	100	705	1,111	900	599	240	46	72
New York	2,101	1,616	1,616	2,200	2,190	380	216	182
Oregon	2,001	808	1,414	500	499	60	103	48
Washington	1,408	2,523	2,222	1,600	1,292	420	75	36
Wisconsin	904	606	707	2,000	998	80	44	
Total in U.S.	16,135	19,789	17,776	13,300	10,755	2,620	1,647	1,402

Note: The IPUMS-USA uses a 1% sample through a 1-in-100 national random sample of the population for the 1910-1930 Census periods. For 1980-2000 Census counts, IPUMS-USA uses a 5% sample or a 1-in-20 national random sample of the population. Source: Author tabulation using http://usa.ipums.org/usa/.

Therefore, research is easier done by using the Public-Use Microdata Samples (PUMS). These files contain records for a sample of housing units with information on the characteristics of each unit and each person in it. While preserving confidentiality (by removing identifiers), these microdata files permit users with special data needs to prepare virtually any tabulation. Ideally, a research project such as Finland-Swedes in Michigan or Finland-Swedes in the United States would employ RDC data. Language allocation among Finland-Swedes would be greatly aided by RDC data, but obtaining access is obviously not easy. This leads to weighing costs versus benefits. As noted earlier, Finland-Swedes in Michigan are best studied through the use of IPUMS-USA data, which is very helpful, albeit limited in accuracy, in presenting a basic overall understanding of the distribution of Finland-Swedes in the state and in the country.

In Canada, scholars have estimated that some 10,000 Finland-Swedes immigrated to the country by 1930.[29] Finland-Swedes first appeared in Victoria,

British Columbia, in 1880 and were followed by others in mining and lumbering towns such as Bralorne, Trail, Nelson, and Port Alberni, as well as Vancouver and New Westminster. Across the Canadian Prairies, Finland-Swedes settled in New Scandinavia and Winnipeg, Manitoba; New Stockholm, Saskatchewan; and Wetaskiwin, Alberta. In the East, Finland-Swedes settled in Port Arthur/Fort William, Sault Ste. Marie, Toronto, Hamilton, and Windsor, Ontario.[30]

Finland-Swedes in Michigan

$\int$ ome of the first people from Finland recorded in Michigan include Fredrick Randall and Fredrika Bremer. Randall was a forty-eight-year-old sailor who was enumerated in the 1850 U.S. Census in Huron County on the shores of Lake Huron.[31] The first Finland-Swede to travel through Michigan also dates to 1850, when Fredrika Bremer visited North America between 1849 and 1851. As noted earlier, an exhibition hall was established in her honor by the American Swedish Heritage Museum located in Philadelphia. Her accounts of travels in which she mentions Lower Michigan were published in the two-volume work titled *Hemmen i den Nya verlden, En dagbok i bref, skrifna under tvenne års resor i Norra Amerika och på Cuba* (Homes of the New World: A diary of two years of travel in North America and Cuba). In this text, Bremer mentions her travels across Lake Erie to Detroit, her overland venture by rail through Ann Arbor to the shores of Lake Michigan, and her eventual crossing onboard a steamer across Lake Michigan to Chicago.[32]

Michigan was one of the first states to attract immigrants from Finland in large numbers. The first immigrants did not, however, come directly from Finland. Several thousand Finns living in Norway, where they were mostly engaged in fishing and mining, followed Norwegians to work in the copper mines of Houghton and Keweenaw counties. It was reported that one mining company sent Christian Taftes to secure miners from Finnmarken and

Tromsø in Norway. In the summer of 1864 he landed in Hancock with over one hundred Norwegians, Swedes, and Finns. Some of the men took up work in the mines, while several were induced to enlist in the U.S. Army, which needed more men in defense of the Union.[33] It is very possible that the first Finland-Swedes arrived in Michigan in this first wave of settlers, and it is recorded that a few Finland-Swedes were found in the Calumet area as early as 1871.[34]

Finland-Swedes closely followed their Finnish-speaking countrymen. Perhaps the earliest arrival of Finland-Swedish immigrants who remained in Michigan dates to 1868 when a group of Finland-Swedes from Chicago settled in Ludington, Michigan, and joined the Emanuel Lutheran Church:

> The first of them was Alex Mattson, an uncle of A. A. Palm arriving in 1868. Two or three years later Matts Borg, John Hakalax and Carl Liljestrom. In 1872 the number was added to by Andrew Newberg, Anders Borg, Abraham Westerlund, Matts Mattson and fifteen more who came with them from Chicago shortly after their arrival from Finland. Others came later. Some of them became fishermen, others worked as did most of the Swedes in the forests during winter and in sawmills in the city in summers. Sometime later came a number of native Finlanders who stayed for a while and then moved elsewhere, all except Jakob Berglund who lived on a farm on the north side of Lincoln River.[35]

As estimated by IPUMS-USA, the 1910 census showed that the number of Swedish-speaking immigrants born in Finland shows Michigan in first place, with 2,905 Finland-Swedes, representing 18 percent of all Finland-Swedes in the country. Michigan was followed by New York, with 2,101 (13 percent), Oregon with 2,001 (12.4 percent), California with 1,605 (9.9 percent), and Washington with 1,408 (8.7 percent).

Although the percentage share of Finland-Swedes in Michigan declined to 14.6 percent in 1930, it maintained its number-one status with most Finland-Swedes in the country until Washington, California, and New York surpassed Michigan.[36] The 2000 census showed that the most populous states with people born in Finland who spoke Swedish were found in California (23.8 percent) and New York (13 percent). According to this definition, Michigan had a total of eighty-two (5.8 percent) individuals in the nation

Table 3. Finland-Swedes in Michigan counties, 1910–1930 as Estimated by IPUMS-USA

County	1910 census		1920 census		1930 census	
	Number	Percent	Number	Percent	Number	Percent
Alger	202	7.0				
Berrien	200	6.9				
Delta			505	15.6	404	16.0
Dickinson			808	25.0	303	12.0
Genesee					202	8.0
Gogebic	903	31.1	505	15.6	505	20.0
Houghton	1,200	41.3	707	21.9		
Iron			505	15.6	606	24.0
Marquette	100	3.4				
Menominee			101	3.1		
Muskegon	300	10.3			404	16.0
Ontonagon			101	3.1		
Schoolcraft					101	4.0
TOTAL	2,905		3,232		2,525	
Total born in Finland	28,676	10.1	34,022	9.5	29,290	8.6

Note: The IPUMS-USA uses a 1 percent sample through a 1-in-100 national random sample of the population for the 1910–1930 census periods. For 1980–2000 census counts, IPUMS-USA uses a 5 percent sample, or a 1-in-20 national random sample of the population.
Source: Author tabulation using http://usa.ipums.org/usa/.

who could be identified as being Finland-Swedes (table 2). Once again, the census data does not account for descendants who may or may not speak Swedish and who are born outside of Finland.

The majority of Finland-Swedes settled in the Upper Peninsula, as they were attracted to the availability of jobs in the mines and forests of the region. Among the best-known and most populous locations for Finland-Swedes in Michigan were Ironwood, Crystal Falls, Dollar Bay, Negaunee, Escanaba, Gladstone, Felch-Metropolitan, Ludington, and Muskegon.[37] Beyond these locations, others became home to the many Finland-Swedes who immigrated to the state over the decades.

Analysis of the Finland-Swedish population by county reveals certain concentrations as well. According to IPUMS-USA data estimates, the strongest

Table 4. Finnish-Born, Swedish-Speaking Populations in Michigan Counties, 1930

County	Total Population	Total born in Finland	% born in Finland	Total Swedish-speaking	% Swedish-speaking	% Finnish-speaking
Alcona	4,989	1	0.0	0	0.0	100.0
Alger	9,327	941	10.1	40	4.3	95.7
Allegan	38,974	2	0.0	0	0.0	100.0
Antrim	9,979	3	0.0	1	33.3	66.7
Baraga	9,168	1,232	13.4	52	4.2	95.8
Barry	20,928	1	0.0	1	100.0	0.0
Bay	69,474	6	0.0	2	33.3	66.7
Benzie	6,587	9	0.1	4	44.4	55.6
Berrien	81,066	11	0.0	3	27.3	72.7
Calhoun	87,043	14	0.0	0	0.0	100.0
Charlevoix	11,981	1	0.0	1	100.0	0.0
Cheboygan	11,502	8	0.1	5	62.5	37.5
Chippewa	25,047	675	2.7	31	4.6	95.4
Crawford	3,097	28	0.9	4	14.3	85.7
Delta	32,280	944	2.9	333	35.3	64.7
Dickinson	29,941	553	1.8	290	52.4	47.6
Eaton	31,728	10	0.0	8	80.0	20.0
Emmet	15,109	2	0.0	1	50.0	50.0
Genesee	211,641	114	0.1	27	23.7	76.3
Gogebic	31,577	3,129	9.9	256	8.2	91.8
Grand Traverse	20,011	41	0.2	5	12.2	87.8
Gratiot	30,252	1	0.0	0	0.0	100.0
Houghton	52,851	5,957	11.3	140	2.4	97.6
Huron	31,132	3	0.0	0	0.0	100.0
Ingham	116,587	43	0.0	3	7.0	93.0
Ionia	35,093	24	0.1	0	0.0	100.0
Iosco	7,517	67	0.9	38	56.7	43.3
Iron	20,805	1,521	7.3	256	16.8	83.2
Isabella	21,126	1	0.0	0	0.0	100.0
Jackson	92,304	22	0.0	0	0.0	100.0
Kalamazoo	91,368	36	0.0	1	2.8	97.2
Kent	240,511	208	0.1	30	14.4	85.6
Keweenaw	5,076	663	13.1	4	0.6	99.4
Lake	4,066	3	0.1	2	66.7	33.3

County	Total Population	Total born in Finland	% born in Finland	Total Swedish-speaking	% Swedish-speaking	% Finnish-speaking
Lapeer	28,348	1	0.0	0	0.0	100.0
Lenawee	49,849	2	0.0	0	0.0	100.0
Livingston	19,274	9	0.0	0	0.0	100.0
Luce	6,528	549	8.4	51	9.3	90.7
Mackinac/Michili	8,783	157	1.8	98	62.4	37.6
Macomb	77,146	68	0.1	0	0.0	100.0
Manistee	17,409	310	1.8	2	0.6	99.4
Marquette	44,076	3,612	8.2	49	1.4	98.6
Mason	18,756	67	0.4	29	43.3	56.7
Mecosta	15,738	3	0.0	1	33.3	66.7
Menominee	23,652	196	0.8	80	40.8	59.2
Midland	19,150	6	0.0	1	16.7	83.3
Missaukee	6,992	36	0.5	3	8.3	91.7
Montmorency	2,814	27	1.0	0	0.0	100.0
Muskegon	84,630	189	0.2	121	64.0	36.0
Newaygo	17,029	34	0.2	16	47.1	52.9
Oakland	211,251	198	0.1	8	4.0	96.0
Oceana	13,805	1	0.0	0	0.0	100.0
Ogemaw	6,595	1	0.0	1	100.0	0.0
Ontonagon	11,114	1,790	16.1	30	1.7	98.3
Osceola	12,806	4	0.0	1	25.0	75.0
Oscoda	1,728	1	0.1	1	100.0	0.0
Otsego	5,554	9	0.2	0	0.0	100.0
Ottawa	54,858	3	0.0	0	0.0	100.0
Roscommon	2,055	13	0.6	13	100.0	0.0
Saginaw	120,717	13	0.0	1	7.7	92.3
Sanilac	27,751	1	0.0	0	0.0	100.0
Schoolcraft	8,451	129	1.5	58	45.0	55.0
St. Clair	67,563	10	0.0	0	0.0	100.0
St. Joseph	30,618	1	0.0	0	0.0	100.0
Tuscola	32,934	5	0.0	1	20.0	80.0
Van Buren	32,637	2	0.0	0	0.0	100.0
Washtenaw	65,530	17	0.0	5	29.4	70.6
Wayne	1,888,946	3,218	0.2	118	3.7	96.3
Wexford	16,827	66	0.4	26	39.4	60.6
Total		27,022		2,252	8.3	91.7

Source: U.S. Census Bureau, 1930 census data available at http://www.heritage.com and http://www.ancestry.com.

Table 5. Finland-Swedes in Michigan Counties, 1930

Alger County	40	Breitung Township	39	Mason City	1
Burt Township		Felch Village	98	*Iosco County*	*38*
(Grand Marais)	9	Felch Township	87	Alabaster Township	18
Munising City	20	Iron Mountain City	32	East Tawas City	16
Munising Township	1	Norway City	27	Oscoda Township	3
Rock River Township	10	Norway Township	3	Wilber Township	1
Baraga County	*52*	Sagola Township	3	*Iron County*	*256*
Baraga Township	10	Waucedah Township	1	Bates Township	3
Baraga Village	35	*Genesee County*	*27*	Crystal Falls City	141
L'Anse Village	7	Flint City	27	Crystal Falls Township	40
Benzie County	*4*	*Gogebic County*	*256*	Hematite Township	18
Crystal Lake Township	3	Bessemer City	30	Iron River City	8
Gilmore Township	1	Bessemer Township	35	Minnard Hills Village	6
Chippewa County	*31*	Ramsey Village	38	Mansfield Township	2
Hulbert Township	3	Anvil Village	4	Mastodon Township	13
Sault Ste. Marie City	26	Erwin Township	8	Stambaugh City	19
Soo Township	1	Ironwood City	110	Stambaugh Township	6
Whitefish Township	1	Ironwood Township	23	*Kalamazoo County*	*1*
Crawford County	*4*	Marenisco Village	4	Schoolcraft Township	1
Grayling Village	4	Wakefield City	4	*Kent County*	*30*
Delta County	*333*	*Grand Traverse County*	*5*	Grand Rapids City	24
Bay de Noc Township	21	Green Lake Township	1	Sparta Township	5
Brampton Township	16	Traverse City	4	Walkerton Township	1
Cornell Township	15	*Houghton County*	*140*	*Keweenaw County*	*4*
Ensign Township	16	Hancock City	21	Ahmeek Mine	2
Escanaba City	108	Laird Township	4	Mohawk Town	1
Escanaba Township	7	Osceola Township	3	Houghton Township	1
Ford River Township	8	Dollar Bay Town	99	*Lake County*	*2*
Gladstone City	118	Portage Township	1	Elk Township	2
Maple Ridge Township	12	Schoolcraft Township	2	*Luce County*	*51*
Nahma Township	2	Stanton Township	5	McMillan Township	3
Wells Township	10	Torch Lake Township	5	Newberry Village	40
Dickinson County	*305*	*Ingham County*	*3*	Peatland Township	6
Breen Township	15	Lansing City	2	Newberry State Hospital	2

Mackinac County	98	Holmes Township	1	Ontonagon Township	7
Clark Township	57	Ingalleton Township	15	Stannard Township	1
Garfield Township	1	Menominee City	15	*Oscoda County*	1
Hendricks Township	2	Meyer Township	5	Greenwood Township	1
Moran Township (Brevort)	21	Nadeau Township	3	*Roscommon County*	13
Portage Township	2	Stephenson Township	1	Gerrish Township	13
St. Ignace City	14	*Midland County*	1	*Saginaw County*	1
St. Ignace Township	1	Midland Township	1	Saginaw City	1
Manistee County	3	*Missaukee County*	3	*Schoolcraft County*	58
Maple Grove Township		Lake City Village	1	Hiawatha Township	3
(Kaleva)	3	Lake Township	2	Inwood Township	3
Marquette County	49	*Muskegon County*	121	Manistique City	30
Ewing Township	3	Casnovia Township	1	Manistique Township	7
Ishpeming City	2	Dalton Township	2	Thompson Township	15
Marquette City	3	Fruitland Township	1	*Washtenaw County*	5
Negaunee City	31	Mooreland Township	2	Ypsilanti Township	3
Negaunee Township	3	Muskegon City	93	Ann Arbor City	1
Republic Township	1	Muskegon Township	10	Ann Arbor Township	1
Richmond Township	4	Muskegon Heights City	10	*Wayne County*	118
Tilden Township	1	Ravenna Township	2	Brownstone Township	3
Wells Township	1	*Newaygo County*	16	Dearborn Township	5
Mason County	29	Wilcox Township	16	Detroit City	94
Ludington City	21	*Oakland County*	8	Ecorse Township	2
Victory Township	3	Pontiac City	1	Gratiot Township	1
Pere Marquette Township	1	Royal Oak City	2	Highland Park City	5
Amber Township	3	Holly Village	5	Livonia Township	2
Custer Township	1	*Ogemaw County*	1	Radford Township	1
Mecosta County	1	West Branch Township	1	River Rouge City	5
Big Rapids City	1	*Ontonagon County*	30	*Wexford County*	26
Menominee County	80	Bergland Township	17	Cadillac City	20
Cedarville Township	4	Bohemia Township	1	Cherry Grove Township	2
Daggett Village/Township	32	Haight Township	1	Haring Township	3
Faithorn Township	4	Matchwood Township	3	Selma Township	1

Source: U.S. Census Bureau, 1930 census data available at http://www.heritage.com and http://www.ancestry.com.

clustering of Finland-Swedes in 1910 occurred in Houghton County, followed by Gogebic County. These two counties accounted for some 72 percent of all the Finland-Swedes in the state (table 3). Many of the Finland-Swedes were employed in the mining and lumbering industries. Ten years later, the 1920 census showed that the strongest concentration of Finland-Swedes was found in Dickinson County where 25 percent of all Finland-Swedes resided, followed by Houghton County with about 22 percent. The cities of Felch-Metropolitan and Foster City are found in Dickinson County, and here many Finland-Swedes were successful lumbermen and farmers.[38]

Using the IPUMS-USA database for initial census information, data revealed that in 1930 the highest concentration was found in Iron County, where 24 percent of all Finland-Swedes resided. The data suggests that there were no Finland-Swedes in Houghton County that year, which is erroneous. Similarly, while no Finland-Swedes were recorded in the IPUMS-USA census data base for Mason County, detailed examination of the 1930 U.S. census showed a total of sixty-four Finland-Swedes and their descendants in Pere Marquette Township, Victory Township, and the City of Ludington. In fact, Ludington's 4th Ward was home to a total of fifty-four Finland-Swedes.[39] It should also be noted that according to IPUMS-USA, Gogebic County was the only county that maintained a Finland-Swedish presence throughout 1910–1930.

The 1930 census also shows no Finland-Swedes in Houghton County. However, a detailed analysis of the 1930 census manuscripts indicates otherwise. While statistical variance accounts for many of the missing values, fluctuations could also be the result of a changing economy and the availability of seasonal employment opportunities such as mining and lumbering. These factors will be examined in later sections that look specifically at the counties, towns, and settlements in the Upper and Lower Peninsulas.

I conducted a much more detailed analysis of the 1930 census data in the fall of 2010 by spending countless hours analyzing Ancestor.com and HeritageQuest Online, which provided images of the original handwritten census tabulations. The results of this detailed analysis provide the first comprehensive study of the distribution of a total of 2,252 Finland-Swedes in the state (see tables 4 and 5; maps 3 and 4). This information is comparable to the IPUMS-USA data discussed above (8.6 percent vs. 8.3 percent of all Finnish-born residents were Finland-Swedes). Obviously, a thorough examination

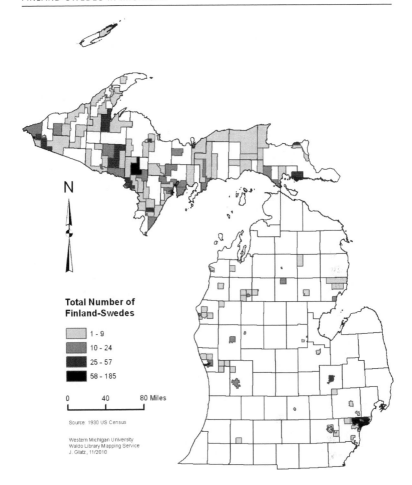

Map 3. Finland-Swedes in Michigan by township, 1930.

and survey of the entire population of the state is more accurate than the 1 percent sample used by IPUMS-USA. Still, in this case the statistical difference in the total population is surprisingly close. However, the geographic difference in distribution is very different, and I will examine this variance in more detail below.

Based on the census manuscript data in table 4, it is noted that for 1930 many more counties had Finland-Swedes when compared to the seven counties reported by IPUMS-USA data (table 3). The data obtained through

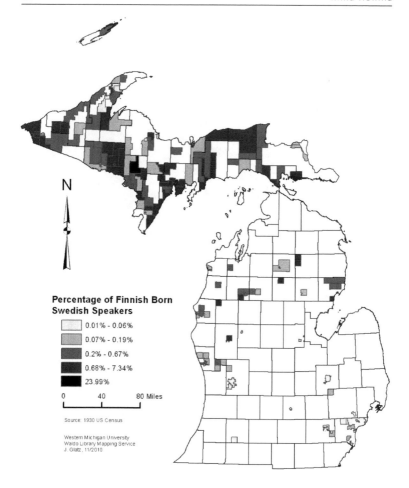

Map 4. Finland-Swedes in Michigan as a percentage of total population by township, 1930.

this analysis is clearly superior to the IPUMS-USA sample, and I will refer to the findings of this data set for the remainder of the text.

The county with the most immigrant Finland-Swedes (born in Finland) was in fact Delta County with 333 individuals, followed by Dickinson County (291), Gogebic County (256), Iron County (256), Houghton County (140), Muskegon County (121), and Wayne County (118). In terms of the most concentrated settlement and highest percentage of Swedish speakers in the entire Finland-born population, several counties with only one Finland-born

Map 5. Past and present locations of Finland-Swedes in Michigan. Source: Adapted from Michigan Finland-Swedish communities as mapped by the Swedish-Finn Historical Society (http://finlander.genealogia.fi/sfhswiki/index.php/Michigan).

resident speaking Swedish provided for a 100 percent Finland-Swedish presence. However, the most significant Finland-Swedish presence was found in Roscommon County, where thirteen Swedish-speakers in Garrish Township represented all Finland-born residents (tables 4 and 5). Of the counties with the highest absolute numbers noted earlier, the highest percentages included Muskegon County (64 percent) and Dickinson County (52.4 percent).

The top five urban settlements included Crystal Falls (141), Gladstone (118), Ironwood (110), Escanaba (101), and Dollar Bay (99) (table 5).

While IPUMS-USA data alleges that no Finland-Swedes lived in Alger, Berrien, Houghton, Marquette, Menominee, and Ontonagon Counties, the 1930 census manuscript analysis clearly indicates that there were many Finland-Swedes living in the area.

Present-day geographic analysis of 100 Michigan towns and cities identified as home to Finland-Swedes indicates that the majority are in the Lower Peninsula, countering the distribution noted historically as being in the Upper Peninsula (see map 5). While the absolute number of Finland-Swedes in the Upper Peninsula has historically been higher than in the Lower Peninsula, the scatter, or number of known locations where Finland-Swedes have been found, includes forty-two towns, villages, and settlements. A lower absolute population of Finland-Swedes has always existed in the Lower Peninsula, but the scatter shows a total of fifty-eight cities, towns, and villages. The difference between the two distribution patterns is explained by clustering, which is more evident in the Upper Peninsula and is supported by the census findings.[40]

Finland-Swedes in the Upper Peninsula

As has already been noted, the Finland-Swedish population in Michigan has always been more evident in the Upper Peninsula. At least forty-two locations with Finland-Swedes are identified in the Upper Peninsula. In this region, the counties and towns with Finland-Swedish settlements included (from the west to the east) Gogebic County (Bessemer, Ironwood, Jessieville, Ramsey, Wakefield); Ontonagon County (Bruce Crossing, Ewen, Ontonagon); Houghton County (Alston, Calumet, Dollar Bay, Hancock, Oskar); Baraga County (Baraga); Keweenaw County (Ahmeek, Isle Royale); Iron County (Alpha, Amasa, Crystal Falls, Iron River, Stambaugh); Marquette County (Champion, Marquette, Negaunee); Dickinson County (Felch-Metropolitan, Iron Mountain, Kingsford, Norway, Quinnesec); Delta County (Cornell, Escanaba, Gladstone); Alger County (Grand Marais, Munising); Schoolcraft County (Manistique, Thompson); Luce County (Dollarville, Newberry); Mackinac County (Brevort, Cedarville, St. Ignace); Chippewa County (Sault Ste. Marie).[41]

The following sections briefly look at the counties with the most sizable Finland-Swedish presence in Delta, Dickinson, Iron, Gogebic, Houghton, and Mackinac counties.

Delta County (Escanaba, Gladstone, and Cornell)

Several Finland-Swedes were living in Escanaba as early as 1880. These included Peter Gullans and Charles Groop, both of whom worked in the railway industry. Gullans was a railroad smith, while Groop was a brakeman on the railroad.[42] Others followed and by the turn of the century the number of Finland-Swedes in the city was calculated to be over 200; the number of women was only about half of that. The majority of people worked in the many surrounding lumber camps during the winter, while in the summer work was found in sawmills or ore mines. Farming was an option that was also available to some, which led to settlements in locations such as Cornell. In the early 1900s, Escanaba became well known for its many boarding-houses, saloons, a community hall, and the establishment of the Scandia Cooperative Association.[43]

According to the 1930 census, Delta County, with its total of 333 Finland-Swedish residents (not including their descendants), was the most dominant county in terms of numbers in the state. The cities of Gladstone (118) and Escanaba (108) also ranked at the top of the list in the state as well (table 6). Of all the Finland-born residents within the county, a total of 35 percent spoke Swedish.

According to Anders Myhrman, several members of the second generation became very successful and well known.[44] One of these included Gunnar Back of Escanaba (1906–1983), who after completing university studies was a teacher of English literature for a time and later became a radio and TV commentator in Washington, D.C. He worked for Columbia Broadcasting Systems and as news chief for the American Broadcasting Company in Philadelphia. He received many awards, including the 1960 Columbia University Award and the Donaldson Award for a documentary on air pollution. He retired in 1971, after which he served as the director of the American Swedish Historical Museum for several years and did voiceover work. In 2004 Gunnar Back was inducted into the Broadcast Pioneers of Philadelphia Hall of Fame.[45]

In Delta County, the city of Gladstone, which is located some twelve miles north of Escanaba on the western side of Little Bay de-Noc, was home to

Table 6. Finland-Swedish Occupations in Michigan, 1921

Location	Dominant occupation
Amasa	Mining and a second job
Bay City	Factory
Baraga	——
Bessemer	Mining
Crystal Falls	Mining and farming
Calumet	Mining
Caspian	——
Dollar Bay	Dockwork, factory, and farming
Detroit	Factory
Escanaba	Various occupations
Flint	Factory
Gladstone	Various occupations
Hancock	Mining
Ironwood	Mining
Iron Mountain	Mining
Ishpeming	Mining
Ludington	Factory, farming, and a second job
Marquette	Various occupations
Munising	Mining
Metropolitan	Farming
Manistique	Mining
Negaunee	Mining
North Escanaba	Mining
Norway	Mining
Ontonagon	Dockwork/stevedore and various occupations
Ramsey	——
Quinnesec	Mining

Source: Johannes Näse, "Finlandssvenskarna i Amerika," in *Svensk-Ostrobottniska Samfundet, Arkiv for Svenska Österbotten*, Band 1, Häfte 3–4 (Vaasa, Finland: F. W. Unggrens Boktryckeri, 1922).

many Finland-Swedes. The main industry was lumbering, along with a port for shipment of iron ore. In the 1890s there was also a coal dock and a corn elevator. Later a chemical plant (for Ford Motor Company), a large veneer factory, and a paper mill also employed many.

The earliest settlers in Gladstone were John Thors and Charles Ryss from Solv, Finland, who arrived in the city in 1887. In the middle of 1904 a census was taken among Finland-Swedes in the city. There were sixty-five families comprising 392 individuals, of which 184 were men, 93 women, and 115 children. These statistics reveal that there were a proportionally large number of men, which was common during the great immigration period.[46] According to the 1930 census, a total of 118 Finland-Swedes were recorded living here.

Gladstone was also home to a restaurant, two butcher shops, a drug store, a hardware store, and starting in 1957 the largest and most modern supermarket in Delta County.[47] There were also two Finland-Swedish doctors who practiced in the city. A large Finland-Swedish population also led to activities in the community and included a temperance society, a women's sewing society, and a male choir named "Eko." During the turn of the century, social activities in the meeting hall catered to the temperance movement, which later evolved into the Order of Runeberg. There were also Lutheran and Baptist congregations.[48]

Of interest is also Cornell, which has a distinct place in Finland-Swedish church history. Perhaps the best way to appreciate Cornell is to hear from local residents themselves.

> My grandfather came to the U.S. I don't know what year, but he went to work in the mines at Quinnesec. Him and his neighbor John Mattson come together and in 1904 they bought the property where we're at right now. They each bought 40 acres side by side and they built a log cabin with sod roof with a hand dug well. They lived together for a couple of years until their families came, and then their families lived together for a year or two until they built the houses. Work back then involved cutting wood in the winter and working on the farm in the summer.[49]

Although a small community, Cornell is recognized for the Swedish-Finn Methodist Church, which was attended by local Finland-Swedes.

The church and Sunday school was across the field [from the Carlson farm]. Rev. Hammer would stop in on Sunday, and in the afternoon he'd stop for supper, and he says "I'm going to get stuff ready, I'll see you all in a half an hour." There was no getting out of church because he saw you there. In that church there were no pews, they had chairs. There was a big stone fireplace in the back, and a kitchen. It was kind of low ground there and I remember the cars pulling up alongside there and they'd get stuck and you'd have to go and push them out of the mud every time they'd pull up beside the church. My grandpa donated the land for the church. I guess the church paid for the transfer title and the legal fees. My grandfather and Dick's grandfather [Richard Blixt]—they hand hewed all the timbers for the church. My dad had a big drill and they drilled with rods down through the timbers, they were concaved and convexed and they'd fit together packed them with oakum. Big rods down through them, wooden maple rods. The church had a fire in the 1980s sometime and was damaged quite a bit. It wasn't a church any more, as it had been sold and people were living in it. And I remember after it burnt, they came with a crane and they tried pulling them logs apart. They couldn't do it. They had to cut them with chainsaws, to get them logs apart, they were pegged so tight together.[50]

In recalling the variation in Swedish language that was spoken among Swedes and Finland-Swedes in Escanaba, third-generation Finland-Swede Clayton Carlson noted that "Grandpa Carlson said, 'I can understand them, but it's different.'" To get away from the farm and head to a big city was problematic for some. The hard life of the immigrant seldom was able to provide for bus fares and other costs. Thus, it was common for many to experience hard work.

I graduated from high school and I wanted to go to Chicago to look for a job. My dad said I don't have the money to give to you. He says—there's the bucksaw and there's the ax he says—go across the road he says. All that nice poplar over there and cut it. In a week's time I cut about 3 cords and I took the wood to the pit mill on Friday and got my check and went down to Chicago on Saturday morning.[51]

Back then the woods were free for cutting, but today such activities require permits and contracts.

As of 2010, although actual numbers are hard to come by, the Escanaba area is still home to a small number of Finland-Swedes, along with some businesses that have a connection to the ethnic group. Several residents attend the Escanaba Central United Methodist Church under the leadership of Rev. Scott Harmon. His church is home to several Finland-Swedes, but there is no connection to the Swedish language or history today.[52]

Dickinson County (Felch-Metropolitan and Iron Mountain)

Historians have long recognized the community of Felch-Metropolitan as being one of the most Finland-Swedish communities in the country. Metropolitan was established in the early 1800s with the discovery of iron ore, and when a railroad spur was constructed from Escanaba in 1882 mining began in earnest. At the same time, logging began in the area and a sawmill was built in 1885. Mining, however, was not very profitable and it shut down at the end of the 1890s. The logging operation felled the best and tallest trees and ceased operations there a few years later.[53]

The Skogs were among the first Finland-Swedish families in Metropolitan. Erik Skog (1848–1926) and his wife, Brita (1852–1927), were both born in Jeppo, Finland. Erik Skog arrived in the United States in 1873 and worked in the Ironwood area a while before Brita arrived. Their first child was born in 1882 in Quinnesec, Michigan, where they lived for several years. In about 1888 they built a house with eleven rooms and seven bedrooms just southwest of Metropolitan. For many years they boarded workers employed by the Metropolitan Lumber Company sawmill, as well as immigrants arriving from Finland. The Skog home was the center of many community activities, and they helped establish the Zion Lutheran Church, which was eventually built 400 feet southeast of their property.[54]

Others followed and the stream of immigrants that was probably the greatest in 1888–1893 ended around 1910. Most of the immigrants came from Jeppo and Purmo, but several other parishes in Ostrobothnia were also represented. Some sent for their wives and children, but most of the immigrants were single young men. Later, single young women arrived, which led to many marriages.[55]

During the time of mining and lumbering, Metropolitan had a population of more than 1,000 that comprised many nationalities. When the two main industries shut down, many of the other nationalities moved away, leaving many Finland-Swedes in the region. There were two or three native Swedish families, as well as many Norwegians and some other nationalities, but the Finland-Swedes were most numerous. When the mining and logging ended, some of the Swedish-Finns began a logging business. They logged maple and cedar and had their own camp, horses, and other equipment. When it turned cold and snowy, they made an ice road so the big loads of logs could be hauled out with horses. The lumber camp housed ten to twenty men who worked on a daily basis or did piecework. A couple of women were cooks in the camp. At the same time, some began to farm and the number increased as time went on.

Farming practices developed slowly. As a result, the lumber camps in the winter probably remained the main source of income for many Finland-Swedes. Still, numerous farmers cultivated 60, 80, and up to 100 acres of land. As a result, Metropolitan became a more typical farming community. John Blomquist, one of the most successful loggers and farmers, began logging in 1896 and continued each winter for about fifty years. In 1942 he owned two sections of wooded land. He had a farm of 470 acres, of which 170 was cultivated. On the farm he sold thirty animals and about 100 tons of hay each year.[56]

According to the 1930 U.S. Census, Felch Township was home to the most concentrated Finland-Swedish population in the state. Felch Township, which included Felch Village, combined for an amazing 24 percent share of the total township population of 771 residents. The total of 185 residents born in Finland and speaking Swedish did not include the children and spouses who were not born in Finland and did not speak Swedish. If these were added, the Finland-Swedish proportion would be much higher. Finally, it needs to be noted that 52 percent of all residents born in Finland spoke Swedish (table 5). In 2000, Felch Township was home to a total of 726 residents. The presence of Zion Lutheran Church of Metropolitan sits almost exactly on the site of the old Metropolitan village site, which is now nothing but a string of farms along the country roads.[57]

Iron County (Crystal Falls and Iron River)

Finland-Swedes settled in Crystal Falls in 1880–1881, with several families becoming farmers. In 1911 Finland-Swedes became involved successfully in the Crystal Falls Cooperative Society.[58] Similar to other locations, a temperance organization was established in the early 1900s, as were the Order of Runeberg and a Lutheran congregation.[59] By 1930 Crystal Falls had a Finland-Swedish population of 141 and was the most concentrated single urban settlement in the state. Other cities in the county included Stambaugh (19), Iron River (8), and Minnard Hills Village (6). Finally, Amasa, some twelve miles north of Crystal Falls, was home to a sizable Finland-Swedish population. After 1900, about 25 percent of Amasa's Finnish population was also Swedish.[60]

Gogebic County (Ironwood and Bessemer)

Gogebic County has always maintained a strong Finland-Swedish presence. Detailed study of the 1930 U.S. Census manuscripts shows that Finland-Swedes were present in large numbers, especially in Ironwood and Bessemer. Ironwood was well known for its mines, which provided work for many men in the area. The daily newspaper—Ironwood News Record—notes many events held in the Swede-Finn Hall, where the Order of Runeberg met, a local city school basketball team played, a lumbermen's strike maintained its headquarters, and the Finn-Swede Congregational Church first met prior to building a church of its own in 1909. According to the detailed 1930 census manuscript count, Ironwood was home to 110 Finland-Swedish immigrants. The majority lived in Precinct 9, where a total of 47 resided. Other areas with a concentration of Finland-Swedes included Precinct 8 (29), and Precinct 4 (16). When all American-born Finland-Swedes are added to the Finland-born immigrants, the total Finland-Swedish population in Ironwood reached 268 individuals.[61]

In 1930 Bessemer was home to a total of 93 Finland-Swedes in Wards 2, 3, and 5. Thirty of these individuals were born in Finland, while others were born in America. When all children and individuals are included, Bessemer Township—including villages of Ramsey (91) and Anvil (11)—was home to a total of 220 Finland-Swedes. Among the Bessemer residents was forty-four-year-old iron mine foreman Carl O. Johnson and forty-nine-year-old Hilma Johnson, who had a total of twelve children. All individuals were recorded on the 1930 census as having a Swedish mother tongue and Finnish origins.[62]

Houghton County (Dollar Bay and Oskar)

The highest concentration of Finland-Swedes appeared in the Upper Peninsula in the early 1900s. From among the many communities home to Finland-Swedes, one of the most notable counties was Houghton. The best-known town was Dollar Bay, where many men worked in sawmills and logging camps. The work in the lumber camps was seasonal, and after the logs were floated to the sawmills in the spring, many of the men took work in the sawmills.[63] Others worked as commercial fishermen at Portage Entry, which once was the premier location for fishing operations before the Portage Ship Canal was built.[64] Local Finland-Swedes in Dollar Bay organized several organizations, including temperance and benefit societies, the Order of Runeberg, and Lutheran and Baptist congregations.[65] The First Lutheran Church is still operational and is recognized as a Swede-Finn Church.[66]

On the western shore of the Portage Ship Canal in Houghton County is the town of Oskar, named after Finland-Swede Oskar Eliasson.[67] Eliasson (b. 1845) immigrated to the United States in 1872 and settled in Houghton County.[68] Starting out in the charcoal business, he later became the biggest lumberman in the area in the 1890s, employing up to 500 men. He was also the village's first postmaster. The small town's school served as a meeting hall for church services and other functions, and various shops, stores, and a public sauna were established. A forest fire and economic depression eventually drove Eliasson to bankruptcy in 1901, and he moved to Cokato, Minnesota, where he died in 1931.[69] According to the 1910 census, District 120 in Hancock Ward 4, which was home to Oskar Eliasson, had a total of eighty-three Finland-Swedes. Many of these included children in families where a Finnish spouse was also present.[70] While Houghton County has often received attention among immigrant scholars, and the Finnish presence is undoubtedly strong, the concentration of Finland-Swedes there was a relatively low 2.4 percent of the entire Finland-born population. While the Finland-Swedish population in Dollar Bay was the highest, with ninety-nine residents, Hancock's Finland-Swedish population had declined from the 1910 census to a total of twenty-one Finland-Swedes.[71]

Mackinac County (Cedarville and Brevort)

Mackinac County is well known for several small settlements inhabited by Finland-Swedes. In 1930, 58 percent of all Finland-Swedes were found in Clark Township, which is home to Cedarville and Hessel (see table 6). Cedarville was founded as a center for lumbering operations in the 1880s. Between 1883 and 1885 it was known as Haynesville. Brothers Emil and Victor Mattson operated a lumber camp in the area prior to 1890. The Mattsons also built a two-story hotel in 1895 and later became businessmen in St. Ignace. Other Finland-Swedes from the Åland Islands joined the community, comprising the majority of the Swedish-speaking people in Cedarville, St. Ignace, and Brevort.[72]

As noted by John Markstrum, women in the early 1900s maintained their Scandinavian culture by continuing with practices such as transforming wool into cloth, and rags into rugs. This included the construction of carpet looms, which may have been used for weaving cloth. A weaving loom built by Andrew Markstrom in 1902 was used for several years until it was stored away for over fifty years. In the 1970s it was brought into use again, this time as a hobby. Mrs. August Markstrom used the apparatus to relive what earlier settlers had experienced.[73]

The village of Brevort has had a strong Swedish presence for decades. However, the town's ethnic identity often shifted with political developments in Europe. According to a current local resident, Lois Movalson, "The Swedes that came to Brevort in the late 1800s and early 1900s never referred to themselves as Finnish-Swedes, just Swedes. The original immigrants never talked of the 'old country,' and my husband (Dave) thought it was so bad over there for them that they never wanted to speak of their life there. . . . Dave's father was born in Åland when Russia had possession and would call himself a Russian-Swede. . . . In the past years, we have referred to the Swedes of Brevort, St. Ignace, and Cedarville as Ålanders."[74]

Brevort is a small village on the north shore of Lake Michigan, some fifteen miles northwest of St. Ignace. It was founded in 1845 by Henry Brevort, a surveyor assigned to subdivide the area. Settlers named a lake, river, township, and village in his honor. Three lots were acquired by Peter Hombach in 1867, but Åland-born Charles E. Gustafson is considered the original pioneer. "He was followed by so many more Swedes, that it became a Swedish colony."[75] Gustafson (1855–1925) is recorded in the 1900 and 1910 census as having arrived in America in 1880 and working as a fisherman.[76]

The 1900 census notes clearly that every "Finland-Swede" was born in Finland, and the country of Finland is thus recorded. However, the 1910 census used the term "Russian Swede," which is still remembered by the local residents. Since Finland became an independent nation in 1917, it was perhaps inevitable that the 1920 census listed all Swedish speakers as being born in Finland. Finland was also identified in the 1930 census, and

Midsummer Celebration in Brevort

The Swedish-speaking immigrants who settled in Brevort, Michigan, at the turn of the twentieth century continued a tradition from their native Åland Islands, located between Sweden and Finland, of celebrating midsummer with a midsummer pole and festivities. After a storm in the 1960s destroyed the original pole, the tradition was discontinued. When the Movalson family of Brevort visited Åland Islands in the 1970s to research family history, they observed many communities celebrating midsummer with the same type of poles. When they returned to Brevort, they were committed to reviving the tradition with the entire community, creating a new pole out of cedar about half the height of the original pole. On top they placed a carved and painted whirligig representing humanity, a wooden whirligig representing the sun, and a wooden rooster, the sun's herald. Below the carvings are four carved and painted sailing boats that spin in the wind, representing the four seasons. Hanging from the cross beams are crowns, colorful strips of cloth made into balls, representing the six days of creation. During the midsummer celebration men gather poplar leaves, and men and women of all ages tie the leaves into bundles and string them in garlands back and forth along the cross beams. Ropes are then attached to the decorated pole, which is then raised by several men pulling on ropes. A local dignitary pounds in a bolt at the bottom holder to secure the pole upright. After listening to women sing Swedish songs and to Lois Movalson give interpretive remarks geared for new visitors, the community continues the celebration with a potluck dinner.

Source: Lynne Swanson, "The Swedish American Community of Brevort, Michigan: 2010 Awardee, Brevort (Mackinac County), Swedish Midsummer Pole and Celebration," *Michigan Traditional Arts Program, Michigan State University Museum*, available at http://museum.msu.edu/s-program/mh_awards/awards/2010SB.html.

that year Brevort was home to a total of ninety-three residents. Of those residents, thirty-four were either born in Finland or in the United States to Finland-Swedish parents. The proportion of Finland-Swedes in the town thus reached 36 percent. Of these residents, 22 percent spoke Swedish. While four of the men were farmers, five Swedish-speaking Finland-Swedish heads of household were involved in the fisheries industry and were identified as proprietors. An additional six people were laborers in the fisheries as well.

Raising the midsummer pole in Brevort, 2002. Photo courtesy of Lois Movalson.

Among the many working on the lake was the Gustafson family, headed by Ernest G. Gustafson (1862–1943), who moved to America in 1883. He and his three sons, August (b. 1895), John (1900–1977), and Alvin (1909–1977), worked together on Lake Michigan.[77] Thirty-two-year-old Jennie Matson, the daughter of a local Finland-Swede, worked as a teacher in the local public school. Finland-born Aily Nuttila was the other teacher in the school. She lived as a boarder in the home of Finland-Swede Carl Carlson.[78] While a few different occupations were found in Brevort in 1930, the commercial fishing industry employed a third of the Finland-Swedish population. The Gustafson brothers still held a commercial fishing license in 1966.[79]

Today, the population of Brevort is about eighty-five people, five of whom are descendants of the early Swedes.[80] The Trinity Lutheran Church is home to some twenty-five members, "most of whom are Swedish. . . . As the town itself goes through many changes, businesses have shut down, once heavily used fishing docks are now broken and barely visible and even the beaches themselves have gone through massive changes from sandy to rocky, the people can look to the church as a reminder of the past and their heritage."[81] The best-known activity among local residents is the midsummer celebration, which won the 2010 State of Michigan Heritage Award.

Finland-Swedish family outing onboard fishing boat in Brevort, early 1920s.
Photo courtesy of Lois Movalson.

Finland-Swedes in the Lower Peninsula

In the Lower Peninsula, Finland-Swedes are spread across numerous counties and locations. From north to south, there are a total of fifty-eight cities and towns: Charlevoix County (East Jordan); Montmorency County (Lewiston); Alpena County (Alpena); Crawford County (Deward, a ghost town); Roscommon County (Roscommon); Grand Traverse County (Bates); Alcona County (Greenbush, Harrisville, Mikado); Iosco County (Alabaster, Au Sable, East Tawas, Oscoda, Tawas City, Whittemore); Arenac County (Alger); Ogemaw County (Rose City, West Branch); Manistee County (Bear Lake, Bretheren, Copemitch, Filer City, Manistee); Wexford County (Boon, Cadillac); Mason County (Custer, Fountain, Freesoil, Ludington, Scottville); Lake County (Baldwin, Luther); Newaygo County (Ensley Center, Grant, White Cloud, Parks); Mecosta County (Big Rapids); Muskegon County (Montague, Muskegon, White Hall); Ottawa County (Grand Haven); Kent County (Cedar Springs, Grand Rapids, Sparta); Montcalm County (Greenville); Eaton County (Grand Ledge); Bay County (Bay City, Essexville); Huron County (Bad Axe); Genesee County (Fenton, Flint); Oakland County

(Drayton Plains); Macomb County (Center Line); Wayne County (Dearborn, Detroit, Garden City, Grosse Pointe); and Washtenaw County (Ann Arbor).[82] Among the counties in the Lower Peninsula, five—Muskegon, Wayne, Iosco, Kent, and Mason—dominate in terms of Finland-Swedes. These counties are considered in more detail below.

Muskegon County

Data from the 1930 census indicates that a considerable majority of all Finland-born residents in Muskegon county were Swedish speaking. The county boasted a total of 121 Finland-Swedes born in Finland, representing 64 percent of all Finland-born residents, among the highest in the state for that year (see table 5). Within the county, the city of Muskegon was home to ninety-three Finland-Swedes. Contrary to scholars who have noted that Montague and White Hall had Finland-Swedes, the 1930 census did not list any Finland-Swedes in these towns. Instead, they had sizable Sweden-born residents.

Several Muskegon city precincts were home to large numbers of Finland-Swedes, which were found predominantly in the northern part of the city. These areas included Precinct 4 (north end along Muskegon Lake nearest to Muskegon River), with twenty-three (25 percent) of the recorded ninety-three residents. Among them was Victor Johnson, who arrived in America in 1902 and worked as a foreman in a Muskegon bus factory. Precinct 1 (north end, directly east of Precinct 4) was home to a total of seventeen residents, and Precinct 13, on the city's west side along Lake Michigan, was home to another fourteen Finland-born residents. The majority of the remaining Finland-Swedes were concentrated in Precincts 14, 15, and 16, with a total of thirty-three (35 percent) residents.[83]

Muskegon Heights is located directly south of Muskegon, and this area was home to a total of ten residents. Among them was Gabriel Johnson (b. 1879), who arrived in America in 1901 and worked as an engineer at a gas plant.[84]

In terms of occupations, it appears that in 1930 many Finland-Swedes worked in local factories and shops. Some were machinists or cabinet makers. Some also held respected managerial and professional posts. Dairy farming was also present.

Wayne County (Detroit)

Although the percentage concentration of Finland-Swedes in Detroit has remained small, the absolute numbers have been in the top ten list. In 1930, for example, the majority of Detroit's Finland-Swedes were found in the western part of the city. More than half of all the Finland-Swedes in Detroit were found in only five city wards. While the ward boundaries near the center of the city follow the historical layout of settlement based on the French long-lot style (long and narrow lots reaching far inland), the most notable clustering of Finland-Swedes was found in Ward 21, in Detroit's far east side, which is not part of this historical layout of the land. Ward 21 was home to a total of twenty-one (22 percent) of the recorded ninety-four individuals in the city. Other locations included Ward 18, in southwestern Detroit, with ten (11 percent), along with three narrow wards near the center of the city—Ward 12 with nine (10 percent); Ward 2, with eight (8.5 percent); and Ward 4, with eight (8.5 percent). Many of these residents were laborers, some of whom worked in the automotive industry. Others were involved in construction as carpenters, and many of the women worked as servants or maids. Some Finland-Swedes were found in professional occupations such as engineering and medical care. This was exemplified by forty-seven-year-old chiropractor Gunnar Wikander, who immigrated to America in 1902 and was married to forty-year-old Martha of German ancestry. The couple lived in Ward 22 and had three children: Mary (fourteen), Douglas (twelve), and Dagmar (almost five).[85] Historically, the Finland-Swedish concentration in Detroit remained quite small compared to Finnish-speaking Finns in the region.

Iosco County

Iosco County is located along Lake Huron on the eastern side of the Lower Peninsula. East Tawas and Oscoda attracted many Finland-Swedish settlers during the 1880s–1890s. During this time, many Finland-Swedes came to work in the forestry industry as lumberjacks and sawmill workers. The population in East Tawas led to the building of their own Lutheran Church in which Swedish services were held every Sunday. With time, the Swedish services declined to only a few Sunday services a year, which the younger generation did not attend. This decline in membership was also the result of limited work opportunities. As the forests were cut, sawmills eventually closed, and many of the Finland-Swedes began to move away from the area. A large number moved to Duluth, Minnesota, for more lumbering work, while others settled down on farms in the local area. A few others remained and found work in other occupations.[86] According to the 1930 census, Iosco County was home to a total of thirty-eight Finland-Swedes. Within this county, East Tawas was home to sixteen Finland-Swedes born in Finland, who lived in Wards 2 and 3. Alabaster Township was home to eighteen Finland-Swedes. Most of these residents were farmers, while many also found work at the U.S. Gypsum Company quarry in Alabaster as drillers or laborers. In East Tawas, some worked as carpenters in the railway shop, and one was an auto mechanic. There was also Alex Haglund (b. 1880), a commercial fisherman who arrived in America in 1894 and lived in Oscoda Township with his wife and five children.[87]

Kent County (Grand Rapids)

Grand Rapids, which was the second largest city in the state in the late 1800s and developed into a major railway junction and a center for furniture industry, was the destination for Finland-Swedes starting in the 1870s. From Grand Rapids, many immigrants ventured to Muskegon, Ludington, and White Cloud in western Michigan. Anders Hassell (b. 1861 in Karleby, Finland) provides a small glimpse of the early immigration to southern Michigan and the working conditions there:

> I left home in 1878. There were 35 of us who traveled together, most from Karleby, but also some from Kronoby. One of the reasons for going away was the new conscription act which had been adopted by farmers. A few women were with the crowd of emigrants, including my aunt. . . . I was one of the eight who had tickets to Muskegon. There I worked for three years in the woods and in sawmills. The working day had been 12 hours, but there was a strike for 10 hours. I then went to Ludington. Soon, the 10-hour days were in both Ludington and Muskegon. Daily salary was usually $1.50. In Ludington, I worked first at a sawmill, then as a servant in a store. I eventually bought my own saloon in 7 years.[88]

At the turn of the century, it was estimated that some seventy-five Finland-Swedes lived in the city. Many of these early residents worked in furniture factories along with other trades. There were no private organizations, and the Finland-Swedes eventually joined the Swedes in several of their associations and activities.[89] By 1930 Grand Rapids was home to a total of twenty-four Finland-Swedes who were spread across the city in all wards. Many worked in furniture factories as cabinetmakers, hand sanders, and night watchmen. Others were tailors, domestic servants, and inspectors for a refrigerator company.[90] Some also found employment in fruit orchards, especially west of the city.[91]

Mason County (Ludington)

According to a historical account of the Finland-Swedes of Ludington, the residents here preferred the term "Swede-Finn." While a distinct Finn Town did develop in the Ludington area, and Finland was thus recognized, the term "Finland-Swede" is not familiar to residents there.

The first "Swede-Finn" to come to Mason County was Alex Mattson, who arrived in 1868. In 1872 came Andrew Newberg, Anders Borg, and seventeen others from Chicago. Many others arrived between 1885 and 1900 to avoid being drafted into the Russian Army. They found work in the sawmills and lumber camps, including Butters Mill and Taylors Mill along Pere Marquette Lake near Ludington. They lived in boardinghouses in Buttersville and the "Island," also known as Finn Town. At the height of its population, some thirty families lived in Finn Town.

The first significant settlement of fishermen in Ludington was on the shore of Pere Marquette Lake, in what is today the Fourth Ward in Ludington. As the lumbermen came in and sought sites for their mills, the fishermen were driven out. As a result, they established fish shanties, ice houses, and a dance hall on the Island. Each shanty had a long dock where they tied their fishing boats. The salt shed of Butters and Peters Lumber Company had an extra long dock where the Pere Marquette steamers tied up while loading salt and fresh fish for shipment to Milwaukee.

In order to remain connected with the city of Ludington, a hand-drawn ferry operated from Taylorsville to the foot of Ferry Street. Children attended school in Buttersville or rowed across the lake to Ludington's First Ward School.

At the turn of the century, most of the fishermen had only sailboats and often fished for lake trout. Depending on the season, the fishermen would set their nets five to ten miles out in Lake Michigan. Catches would average between 200 and 300 pounds, and fish were sold from five to six cents per pound. The fish were iced in barrels and shipped by boat to Milwaukee and Chicago markets. The nets were lifted by hand. In the early 1900s, gas fishing boats had mechanical aids to lift the nets.

Among the Swede-Finns who became fishermen at the turn of the century were Andrew Newberg; Andrew Borg; Andrew Gustafson; Leander Johnson; Matt Anderson; John Gustafson; Charles J. Johnson; Emil Bishop; Matt Lindquist, followed by his sons, Fred, Alec, and Hugo; Alexander Holmstrom, followed by his sons, Axel, Oscar, and Ernest; and John Johnson, followed by his sons, Frank and Fred.

There was no fishing in the winter months when the ice blocked the channel. Many of the men went back to work in the lumber camps, and others found work in the sawmills and freight sheds.

Mr. Charles J. Johnson came to Ludington in 1891 and was married to Miss Ida Mattson in 1902. Their marriage was celebrated with a big reception in the dance hall on the Island. Mr. and Mrs. Johnson were the last of the fisherfolk to leave the Island, moving to their new home on West Loomis Street in 1910. Prior to this time, all of the others had moved to the mainland to enjoy more modern conveniences, and for their children to be nearer the schools they were attending. Most of them built their homes on West Loomis Street.

The Island remained the center of fishing operations for many years after the families left. Fish shanties continued to be used, and boats were tied up at the adjoining docks.

Swede-Finns found work at Stearns Mill, Wards Mill, Anchor Block (forerunner of the Morton Salt Company), and a basket factory. Many lived in Ludington's Fourth Ward, and some gained leadership positions as ward commissioners and members of the Swedish Aid Society. As with other ethnic groups, the Swede-Finns found the church the center of their social activities. The women were active in the Ladies Aid, while many men served on the church council of the Emanuel Lutheran Church.[92]

Newaygo County (White Cloud)

Smaller concentrations of Finland-Swedes were found in White Cloud, Newaygo County. The U.S. Census Bureau records several people born in Finland and living in Newaygo County in 1870, including farmer Hendrick and his wife, Lena Sutherland, along with farm laborer Haugel Martz in

Ensley Center. The village of Newaygo was home to millwright Charles Storm and his family, which included his wife, Mary, and their three children, ages thirteen, ten, and six, who were born in Finland, plus a two-year-old born in Michigan in 1868.[93] According to Anders Myhrman, "hundreds of Swede-Finns worked in the lumber camps and mills in the 1890s and many became farmers there."[94] According to more reliable accounts, the Finland-Swedes did not become farmers but found employment on the railroads when their lumbering days were over.[95] White Cloud was formerly known as Morgan Station and is located approximately fifty miles north of Grand Rapids. A railroad line built specifically for the lumber industry ran between White Cloud and Grand Rapids in 1881.

Swedish-speaking immigrants from the coastal areas of Ostrobothnia found White Cloud to their liking, and one of the earliest arrivals may have been Matts Forstrom, who arrived in White Cloud, Michigan, in 1880. Matts's brother Anders settled in White Cloud by about 1884 and lived in White Cloud and Grand Rapids his entire life. His other siblings, Karl and Johanna, also settled in White Cloud. Johanna married Carl Brandt in White Cloud.[96]

A sizable Finland-Swedish community developed along several streets in southeast White Cloud, and this area became the nucleus of "Swedetown." The Utters were one of the best-known families. Born in Uttermossa, Finland, Viktor Utter arrived in White Cloud in 1882 and was married to Emma Ljung-kvist. Emma was the daughter of highly respected Swedish boardinghouse owner Charlotta Ljungkvist, who arrived from Östergötland, Sweden, about 1880. Along with owning a farm east of town for several years, and relocating to White Cloud and establishing a career with the railways, the Utter family was well known for the orchestra it formed with their eleven children, who were born between 1889 and 1914. According to local newspaper clippings, the family was very musical, and the children performed at parades, private festivals, military reunions, and dances.[97]

White Cloud's Finland-Swedes built houses, became active in the Swedish Mission Church and assimilated into the Swedish community. Many of their descendants remained in White Cloud and became active and respected citizens.[98] Several of the homes built by these immigrants have undergone extensive remodeling, and some of the Swedetown houses are still standing. The Swedish Mission Church building was sold to a hunting club and moved to a location about fifteen miles northeast of White Cloud, after the property came under ownership of Newaygo County. Many of the Swedetown homes have been torn down—replaced by county government buildings, gas stations, and restaurants. None of the White Cloud business buildings in which the Swedish immigrants found work still stand. Less than a half dozen of the original Swedetown families still remain in the White Cloud area.[99]

Finland-Swedish Organizations

Along with other ethnic groups that immigrated to America looking for a new life in the "Promised Land," where opportunities for economic success were plentiful, many Finland-Swedes were often at a loss when their plans and hopes were dampened by harsh work conditions, illness, and untimely death. Although many immigrants brought little organizational pattern or background to combat these problems, they soon established several organizations that helped thousands of Finland-Swedes across the country. The first was Imatra, a benefit society, in 1889, followed by the temperance society Aavasaksa in 1892. Both were established in Worcester, Massachusetts. Interestingly, the first benefit or temperance society in Michigan was founded in Metropolitan in 1892.[100] However, the temperance society Morgonstjärnan (Morning Star) in Ironwood on January 30, 1898, and the benefit society Österbotten in Bessemer on April 16, 1898, initiated a movement to form not only new local societies but also associations of societies. The societies in Bessemer and Ironwood became the leaders in their respective associations.

In the following year, benefit societies were founded in Ironwood, Negaunee, and Crystal Falls. Representatives of the four societies met in Bessemer on February 5, 1900, and organized the Swedish Finnish Benefit Association (Svensk-Finska Sjukhjälpsförbundet). This association grew slowly for a few years, but later its progress was rapid. In 1915 there were thirty-eight local societies with 2,237 members, and in 1920 the membership of fifty-one active local societies was about 3,500. Of these fifty-one societies, five were located in the East, twenty-eight in the central states, six in the mountain states, and eleven on the West Coast.[101] Michigan was home to several societies established in Bessemer (1898), Ironwood (1899), Negaunee (1899), and Crystal Falls (1899). Other Michigan locations included Calumet, Dollar Bay, Gladstone, Iron Mountain, Escanaba, Baraga, and Metropolitan.[102]

The emphasis of the Sick Benefit Association was focused primarily on aid and benefits for individuals and families in times of illness, accidents, or deaths; however, social and cultural activities were important as well. According to the constitution of the association, its purpose was

> to bring together in brotherly harmony persons speaking Swedish or Finnish without respect to religious or political views, to promote amity, friendship, and helpfulness, to gather collectively means to aid members who are ill or who have through illness or accident become incapable of working, to pay funeral benefits on the death of members, and to seek in other ways to promote harmony and the feeling of brotherhood among our countrymen in this land.[103]

After the founding of temperance society Morgonstjärnan in Ironwood in 1898, the idea of temperance gradually took hold. Within four years, fifteen temperance societies were formed, the majority in the Upper Peninsula of Michigan, only to be founded alongside benefit societies that were also found in many towns and cities of the region. The temperance societies first joined the Finnish National Brotherhood, but on November 20–21, 1902, representatives from eleven of these temperance societies met in Crystal Falls and organized the Swedish Finnish Temperance Association (Svensk-Finska Nykternetsförbundet). The association began with sixteen societies and about 500 members, but it grew quickly in the following years. In 1908 there were fifty-one active local societies with some 2,100 members. The growth of the society slowed down over the following years, and by 1917 there were sixty societies with a membership of about 2,600. Of these societies, eight were located in the East, thirty-one in the central states, seven in the mountain states, and fourteen on the West Coast. [104] In 1917 Michigan was home to nineteen temperance societies, representing almost two-thirds of all the chapters. Temperance societies were established in Ironwood (1898), Bessemer (1898), Negaunee (1898), Amasa (1899), Crystal Falls (1899), Gladstone (1899), Ludington (1899), Felch (1900), Dollar Bay (1902), Escanaba (1902), Quinnesec (1903), Ramsey (1903), Baraga (1903), Thompson (1906), Jessieville (1908), Hancock (1909), Manistique (1911), Munising (1912), and Newberry (1915).[105]

Most of the work of the Swedish Finnish Temperance Association was educational, with informative and entertaining programs and social activities to promote temperance. For this reason, many of the societies built their own halls. Women's auxiliaries (sewing societies), choirs, and brass bands were also part of the temperance movement.[106]

The Temperance Association sponsored three publications. The monthly paper *Ledstjärnan* (*Leading Star*), began in January 1906. Two other publications celebrated the association's history and numerous lodges. Both publications are valuable for their historical content and photos depicting the period.[107]

Over time it became obvious that there was some overlapping of memberships and duplication of activities, which led to the merger of the Temperance Association and Sick Benefit Association associations. While some societies declined to form a unified organization, the founding of the Order of Runeberg ultimately helped to bring the Finland-Swedish communities closer together.

The Order of Runeberg

A complete merger of the benefit and temperance associations took place in 1920 with the founding of the Order of Runeberg. The new fraternal order left the beneficial provisions intact, but the temperance requirement was considerably modified. All benefit lodges joined the new Order of Runeberg, but ten temperance lodges, apparently dissatisfied with the temperance statement in the constitution, refused to join. Five of these were located in the East, where the opposition to the merger had been the greatest.[108] Temperance lodges in Amasa, Ludington, Quinnesec, Thompson, Jessieville, and Newberry decided not to join the Order of Runeberg.[109]

While the new organization started with about 4,500 members, the activities

An Order of Runeberg Member

I was born in Dollar Bay in 1924 and lived there all my life, except for a hitch in Milwaukee, from 1948 to 1953, and then I came back to Dollar Bay. I've been in Dollar Bay ever since.

I joined the Order of Runeberg in 1953 and quit in about 1987. I joined because all the young people were joining then at the time, for the social aspect of it, and all my friends were joining, so that's why I joined.

There was entertainment on the weekend. We'd hire music and have dances till maybe twelve or one o'clock, and summertimes we have our annual picnics and then at Christmas we'd have pageants for the kids. We did a lot of work. The basement wasn't completed then, and we completed that while I was a member. And we did maintenance on the main floor, so we had it in good shape for the rest to have.

My parents were [members] there. You see, I think that place was built, I think it was around 1904 or something, and that's when they belonged, and it was a social club then, and they would have their doings. We young people took over in 1948, and only older members were there, and they wanted the younger people to take over. Ted Holm was one of our members that did most of the work getting the place going, and it grew up to around one hundred.

[My parents] emigrated from Finland. They were born in Wasa, like all the Swedish in Dollar Bay, and they came over in 1890 or so—emigrated over here and landed in Dollar Bay. They considered themselves Swedish. Where they came from in Sweden there was no Finland; it was all Sweden. So when they came from there it was all Sweden.

My parents never mentioned much about the homeland. I was born in 1924, so they'd been over here about thirty years then. They did mention that when

of the order flourished, and its influence became most extensive during the 1920s and 1930s, when membership across the country reached 8,000.[110]

As noted earlier, *Ledstjärnan* was started in 1906 by the national temperance society Nykterhetsforbundet to promote its work and that of the temperance movement in general. The paper's contents largely consisted they first came over housing was scarce, so there would be one family down-stairs and one upstairs. The family grew fast because of a smelter, a wire mill, and a sawmill. My grandfather worked in the smelter till it closed and sort of retired after that, I suppose.

They [parents] probably knew Swedish when they came over, but they adapted right away. But the older people would talk Swedish, and my mother and father would talk with them, but it wasn't long, though, when the second generation died off, so there was very little Swedish spoken, so there was no-body left to talk Swedish, so it wasn't long before very little was spoke. The Finns, on the other land, stayed more with their language. I think that was be-cause they came over later. I know when I started school there was two of them, and they couldn't speak a word of English, but they picked it up pretty quick.

There was no tension between the Finns and Swedes. There were more Finns that came over here than Swedes, and the Swedes more or less ended up as farmers, and the Finns did also, but a lot of them went into mining. Their wives would stay and run the farm, you know, as far as milking the cows and all that stuff. The Swedes ended up more as farmers, and the Finns ended up more as miners. A lot of Swedes worked in the lumber mills and smelter by the hour, and then they did some farming as well. The Runeberg Society was made up of typically laborers. Nobody that had any education—they went through high school probably. These other ones that came from Sweden had very little edu-cation. Usually people had very little education. Today, the Order of Runeberg is dwindling down to nothing, so now it's more active on the West Coast. We are the only one that has our own building. All the rest of them, they have their meetings and they rent a place. Way out west they don't own it. I know a lot of them would have their meetings in the houses.

Source: Anders Gillis interview with Harry Nye, Dollar Bay, Michigan, August 23, 2009.

of articles on alcohol and temperance problems, and letters and commu-nications from the local societies. Most of the time it was published as an eight-page monthly, half the size of ordinary newspapers.[111] When the Order of Runeberg was established in 1920, it took over *Ledstjärnan* as its promo-tional organ, and it is still published today.

The Wasa Band of Dollar Bay, Michigan, early 1900s. Myhrman Collection, Åbo Akademi Archives, Åbo (Turku), Finland.

Members of the Swedish Finnish Temperance Association of America Morning Star Lodge No. 1 in Ironwood, Michigan, circa 1913. Myhrman Collection, Åbo Akademi Archives, Åbo (Turku), Finland.

Orchestra of Morning Star Lodge No.1 in Ironwood, Michigan, circa 1913. Photo courtesy of Svea Clayton, Ludington, Michigan.

Members in front of the Österbottens Hall in Negaunee, early 1900s. Myhrman Collection, Åbo Akademi Archives, Åbo (Turku), Finland.

Today the Österbottens Hall is beautifully restored and serves as the office for a Negaunee businessman. Photo by Arnold Alanen, Madison, Wisconsin.

At the height of its success, the Order of Runeberg maintained lodges in Michigan, mostly in the Upper Peninsula. Today, Dollar Bay is the only active lodge among the many Michigan Runeberg lodges. Of the remaining twelve active lodges across North America, it is the last lodge to maintain and use its own lodge building. Since its founding in 1902, the lodge has remained an active cultural, historical, and social organization.[112] In 2010 the lodge had sixty-four members.[113]

Work Life

In the American Midwest, most of the newcomers from Finland initially found economic opportunities in the lumber or mining industries. Southern Michigan attracted loggers and sawmill workers in the 1870s and 1880s. Once the forests had been cut, many moved to the north, where mining provided work. When the mines in Michigan did not provide employment, Finland-Swedes were known to move to Minnesota to continue their trade.[114]

Perhaps the best example of the attraction of the lumber industry is Deward, Michigan. While researching church membership records in Ludington, it became clear that many men relocated to take up work in Deward,

Suicide in Mine

Charles Runeberg, a miner at the East Norrie, committed suicide in the mine Wednesday night. The method employed by Runeberg was unusual and novel, consisting of the placing of a stick of dynamite in the collar of his working-jacket, to which was attached a short piece of fuse. A match was applied to the fuse, the dynamite exploding almost instantly, and the man's head was blown to fragments.

Runeberg worked with Victor Anderson in room 41, 13th level, No. 3 shaft East Norrie Mine. He was a hard drinker, and had been away from work for a week on one of his periodical sprees, returning to work Wednesday evening. He helped Anderson drill three holes and break some "dirt." About ten o'clock he said he was tired and went out to the drift. Runeberg not returning within a reasonable time, Anderson went to look for him. Shift Boss Axel Erickson and Andrew Aperson, a timberman, joined in the search, and the missing man was finally located in an unused drift leading to the Aurora mine. As Anderson and Aperson came to the drift, they started toward Runeberg, who was lying on the ground some distance away. As they approached him, Runeberg, who appeared to be smoking his pipe, lighted the fuse attached to the dynamite with his candle. Anderson and Aperson were horrified at the man's act, and realizing that an attempt on their part to save Runeberg would probably cost them their lives, turned and fled to a place of safety. The fuse was only a few inches in length, and the two men had barely turned into an old room when the dynamite exploded. He had placed the dynamite behind the collar of his working-jacket, and his head was blown off.

Runeberg was thirty-three years old, a Swede-Finn, single, and had worked in the mines of Ironwood for ten years. He was a powerful man, and was said to be one of the best miners in the city, his one failing being his desire for liquor. Coroner Houle has impaneled a jury and will hold an inquest next Wednesday.

Source: "Miner Commits Suicide," *Ironwood News Record*, December 28, 1908.

which today is a ghost town northwest of Frederick along the Manistee River in Mancelona Township, Antrim County. A total of six Finland-Swedish member families from the Emanuel Lutheran Church moved from Ludington to Deward in 1903, followed by one more family in 1904, representing thirty-four individuals.[115] With many families and children, Deward, named after the lumbering baron David E. Ward, was a vibrant logging community of 800 people. The Deward post office was established in 1901, in addition to a school, church, community hall, boardinghouse, hotel, and stores. There was also a roundhouse for train, depot, warehouse and other facilities connected with the Detroit & Charlevoix railroad yards, over which eight engines steamed day and night, delivering nearly one-quarter of a million board feet of lumber, the daily output of the sawmills. The sole purpose of the town was to liquidate Ward's Michigan lumber assets, as directed in his will following his death. Hundreds of thousands of acres of white pine grew in the surrounding forests, and a mill was constructed. At the time, the mill was a state-of-the-art facility designed by the finest German engineers. Ward's property was successfully logged off and required ten years to complete. By 1910 the logging industry was in decline, and the mill closed in 1912. By 1917 most of the people had left.[116]

Iron Mountain, Negaunee, and Ironwood were home to many Finland-Swedes in the mining industry. Smaller numbers worked in manufacturing and the building trades. In a few places farming and fishing quickly became chief occupations. A well-known Finland-Swedish farming community existed in Metropolitan. Commercial fishing among Finland-Swedes was confined to the Great Lakes—namely Lake Superior and Lake Michigan. Excellent examples of Finland-Swedish commercial fishing operations were found in Ludington, Manistee, and Ontonagon.[117]

A valuable contribution was made by Johannes Näse in 1922, when he studied the economic distribution of Finland-Swedes throughout the continent for the early 1920s.[118] His study was based on a questionnaire survey of 713 Finland-Swedes throughout the United States, which helped establish the numerous areas of settlement, as well as detailing the dominant occupations among Finland-Swedes in each area. Näse comprised a list of fourteen occupational groups that were representative of the time period. The most dominant occupations across the country included mining (18 percent), carpentry and construction (17 percent), factory workers (14 percent), farmers (14 percent), and lumberjacks and sawmill workers (11 percent). These occupations account for 74 percent of all occupational categories associated with the surveyed population.[119] For Michigan, mining is the most dominant occupation. A total of fourteen (52 percent) cities and towns out of a total of

Skoog Hardware Store

Skoog Hardware Store at 307 South James Street has been one of Ludington's mercantile establishments since 1910. W. J. Skoog (Pep to his friends), the present proprietor, is a son of Charles Skoog, one of the partners who founded the business. The firm of Skoog & Borg was organized in 1910. The partners Charles Skoog and Herman Borg opened a new hardware store in the Johnson block of South James street. Mr. Borg, who had worked for some time previous in the Goodsell (Ackersville) hardware store, was at first the only one of the partners to devote his full time to the business. Mr. Skoog, who had been a lumber inspector to the mills and a carpenter by trade, continued on at his carpenter work. Ten years later, in 1920, Charles Skoog quit his carpentering to devote his full time to the store along with his son Herman Skoog, who in 1919 had bought Mr. Borg's interest in the business.

In 1916 the stock of merchandise had been moved into the Blumenstock block of South James Street, and in 1932 was moved again to the present location of the store. Father and son continued their partnership until it was broken by the death of Herman Skoog in 1933. Pep, the youngest brother, had grown up in the business, helping at times in the store and while a youth had also worked as a carrier boy for the Ludington Daily News and was later employed in the mailing room of the newspaper for a time. He worked with his father and brother in the store from 1922 on through 1933 and then for sixteen years was employed outside the business.

On the death of Charles Skoog in 1948, W. J. Skoog took over the hardware business and has since devoted his full time to the store. Shelf hardware, household supplies, paints, and numerous miscellaneous hardware items are stocked in the Skoog store. A tin shop is operated in connection with the business. In 1949, Mr. Skoog bought the building in which his store occupies the street floor. On the second floor are living rooms where he resides with his family.

Editor's note: Today the business remains on South James Street and is called Skoog Heating and Cooling. It was taken over in 2000 by fourth-generation descendant Mike Skoog, a forty-seven-year-old entrepreneur who notes that the original family name was changed from Alskog to Skoog when great-grandfather Charles arrived in America (interview with Mike Skoog, Ludington, Michigan, March 4, 2010).
Source: Leonore P. Williams, "Skoog Hardware Store Has Been City Mercantile Establishment since 1910," *Ludington Daily News*, Oct. 7, 1955, 1.

Mike Skoog, third generation entrepreneur in Ludington, Michigan. Photo by author.

Resting place of Charles Skoog in Lakeview Cemetery, Ludington, Michigan. Photo by author.

John and Charles Strandholm commercial fishing with nets on Lake Superior at Hessel, 1900. John A. Markstrum file in Myhrman Collection, Åbo Akademi, Åbo (Turku), Finland, 2010.

twenty-seven locations were dominated by the mining industry. Other notable occupations included factory occupations (five locations) and farming (four locations) (see table 6).

Seasonal employment was also common for many people. When logging was finished, men moved to work in sawmills. Others complemented their livelihoods by fishing on the Great Lakes. Some established businesses that have remained in operation for several generations. A good example of this is Skoog Hardware in Ludington.

Seasonal employment also included fishing. Finland-Swedes fished commercially in all the Great Lakes, with the exception of Lake Ontario.[120] While Ludington's Finn Town was home to many fishermen who trolled the waters of Lake Michigan, Lake Superior and Lake Huron also provided employment for many. Other fishing operations could be found in Muskegon, Cedarville, Hessel, St. Ignace, Brevort, Escanaba, Grand Marais, Munising, and Ontonagon. Perhaps best known were the commercial fishers who spent winters along the North Shore of Minnesota and moved to Isle Royale during the ice-free season.[121]

Church Life

Finland-Swedes became associated with the Lutheran Church in the United States early on. Many of the Finland-Swedish Lutherans joined the congregations associated with the Swedish Augustana Synod organized in Clinton, Wisconsin, in June 1860. The Augustana Church has been identified by several different names over the years. It was called the Scandinavian Evangelical Lutheran Augustana Synod in North America, 1869–1894; Evangelical Lutheran Augustana Synod in North America, 1894–1948; and the Augustana Evangelical Lutheran Church, 1948–1962.[122] In 1962, it merged with Lutheran Churches in America, and since 1988 it has been part of the Evangelical Lutheran Churches in America (ELCA).[123]

It is surprising that the earliest Lutheran congregations among the Finland-Swedes first appeared in Michigan. According to research into the Lutheran congregations, it appears that Grand Rapids had the earliest Lutheran congregation.[124] A group of fourteen Finland-Swedes met at the home of John Newberg on April 13, 1873, and organized the Swedish Lutheran Congregation, adopting the constitution of the Augustana Synod.[125] On April 25, 1874, the congregation was incorporated. Services were held at the Newberg home until the church was built. The Swedish language was spoken until 1919, when English was offered in the second Sunday service. In 1931 English became the only language spoken during services. Today the church is known as Bethlehem Lutheran Church, and many descendants of the Newberg family still attend regularly.[126] According to one member, "If you were Swedish and you moved to Grand Rapids and wanted to work, you first joined the Bethlehem Lutheran Church."[127] The church peaked in 1961 and was the center of social life. Today that is no longer the case. Membership continues to change, but at present some 15 percent of the congregation traces its roots to Swedish roots.[128]

While "churchly activities" were held in Ludington in 1872 amongst the Finland-Swedes and other Scandinavians, the organization of a Lutheran Church happened on August 3, 1874, when the Swedish Evangelical Lutheran Church was founded by twenty-three families. Services were given in Swedish and Norwegian, and by the early 1880s immigration from Sweden and the Swedish population of Finland had brought a "considerable number of Swedish speaking people" to the congregation.[129] Church membership

The current site of Bethlehem Lutheran Church in Grand Rapids, first established 1874. Photo by author.

records indicate that the earliest Finland-Swedes to join the congregation were the Mats Matson family in 1882. Matson (b. 1849 in Kronoby) arrived the United States in 1872 and joined the congregation with his wife, Lovisa (b. 1844 in Nedervetil) and children Matts (b. 1878 in Lincoln) and Ida (b. 1881 in Ludington).[130] From all the records available at Emanuel Lutheran Church, data shows that Finland-Swedish membership grew steadily from 1882 until 1909. The highest annual increases occurred in 1895 and 1896, when twenty-nine and twenty-two members respectively joined the church. A total of forty-five Finland-Swedes transferred their church membership from Finland to Emanuel Lutheran Church between 1882 and 1920, which is 18 percent of all transfers recorded.[131] Today, some fifteen to twenty Finland-Swedish families attend the church, which currently is home to some 192 families.[132]

Lutheran congregations were also established in the Upper Peninsula, and in 1895 Lutheran congregations were founded in Metropolitan and Thompson. Metropolitan joined the Augustana Synod in 1902.[133]

Finland-Swedes in Dollar Bay organized the Finnish Swedish Evangelical Lutheran Church in 1900. The church was constructed in 1902 under the

Emanuel Lutheran Church, Ludington, Michigan. Photo by author.

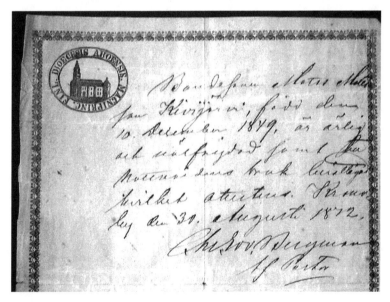

Oldest church transfer certificate from the diocese of Turku. "Farmer's son Matts Mattsson, from Kivijärvi born December 10, 1849, is honest and has a good reputation, furthermore he is entitled to partake in the holy communion, which is confirmed in Kronoby, August 30, 1872. Chr. Erik. Bergman, Pastor." Photo by author.

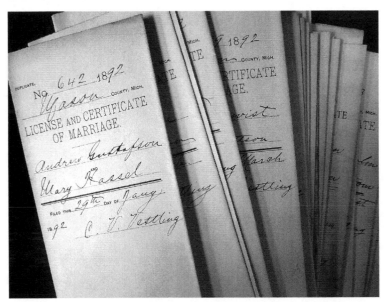

Historically significant marriage licenses and certificates stored in the archives of Emanuel Lutheran Church, Ludington, Michigan. Photo by author.

leadership of Matt Sved and joined the Augustana Synod. Services were conducted in Swedish until 1930, when English became a second language, and the name of the church was changed to the First Lutheran Church. By 1940 the English language was used in all services. Membership records of the congregation exemplify the dominance of Finland-Swedes. Some 90 percent of all the 163 immigrant members were from the Finnish province of Vaasa, with the earliest Finland-Swede, Edvard Ny of Mustasaari (Korsholm), arriving in Dollar Bay in 1887.[134]

Zion Lutheran Church in Ironwood was organized in 1908 and built a sanctuary in 1912. Among the pastors of this congregation were Carl J. Silversten, born in Närpes in 1879, and Frans E. W. Kastman, born in Övermark in 1881. Both pastors served other Finland-Swedish congregations at various times. The pastor of the Ironwood church also served a small congregation in Bessemer. In Brevort, there was a small congregation composed mostly of immigrants from the Åland Islands. It was served by Augustana pastors who lived in Newberry. In 1930 the total membership of the Metropolitan, Dollar Bay, Ironwood, Bessemer, and Brevort congregations was about 800.

Other locations in which some 75 percent of the congregation were Finland-Swedes were found in Crystal Falls and Escanaba.[135]

Finland-Swedes also founded several other congregations based on their religious interests, and some of these were found in Michigan as well. These include the Baptist, Covenant, and Congregational churches, all of which were more common in Sweden and among Swedish-Americans than in Finland and among the Finnish-Americans.

The first Baptist church for Finland-Swedes was organized in Worcester, Massachusetts, in 1900.[136] In 1901 a local mission society in Chicago comprised both Finland-Swedes and Finns and became known as the Finska Baptist Missionsforeningen, or Finnish Baptist Mission Union of America. The primary aim of the mission was to sending out evangelists and missionaries to preach the gospel of Jesus Christ to the Finnish people, using both the Finnish and Swedish languages. The First Finnish Baptist Church was founded in Chicago in 1902 and became Bethel Baptist Church in the 1930s.[137]

The first Baptist preacher among the Finns in the United States was Rev. Matts Esselström (1868–1949), who arrived in Grand Rapids in 1889. He spent the first four years in secular work, but in 1893 he began work as a lay preacher in Bailey, Michigan. In 1895 Esselström pastored in Ludington at the Washington Avenue Baptist Church (later Cornerstone Baptist Church). In 1896 he left Ludington to begin pastoral studies at the Swedish Baptist Seminary in Morgan Park, Illinois. After graduating in spring 1900, Esselström helped organize the Baptist Church of Felch, Michigan, in October 1900 (later Mountain Bible Chapel), and the Swedish-Finnish Baptist Church in Negaunee in August 1902 (later Calvary Baptist Church). He returned to pastor in Negaunee in 1929–1930. Esselström is also well remembered for his role as editor of the *Finska Missionposten* (*Mission Post*), for twenty-seven years. At its height, some 1,300 copies were printed.[138]

In 1916 a total of fifteen congregations with almost 700 members were part of the Baptist Mission Union across the country, with six congregations found in the central states, exemplified by a Finland-Swedish congregation in Gladstone.[139] In the 1930s, five congregations were found in Michigan: Dollar Bay, Felch, Gladstone, Negaunee, and Roscommon.[140]At the annual meeting in 1947 the word "Finnish" was dropped and the official name was changed to "The Baptist Mission of America."[141] By 1957 there were a total of eighteen congregations, with a total membership of over 1,000. The churches were determined to preach the gospel to the Finnish people who spoke Swedish and also to those who spoke Finnish. More than a dozen missionaries were sent out, most of whom spoke both Swedish and Finnish. Many of the churches that grew out of their work were Swedish-speaking, but several congregations spoke Finnish as their language of choice.

A Congregational church was also found in Ironwood. A mission was started during the summer of 1908 among the Finland-Swedes of the region by theological student Mr. H. Granlund. This mission work was continued by the Rev. J. W. Anderson, who had succeeded in organizing a congregation under the name of Finn-Swedish Congregational Church. The Oliver Iron Mining Company donated an empty lot for a new church building, which the society completed in 1909. While the church was under construction, the mission society held its meetings in the Swede Finn Temperance Hall.[142]

In the United States, as in Finland, the relationships between the Swedes and the Finns was sometimes touchy. The Finnish-speaking Finns regarded the Swede-Finns as different and privileged, and the immigrants from Sweden felt the Swede-Finns were not truly Swedes.

Swede-Finns met for fellowship and to learn what was going on in the Old Country. Societies that promoted temperance and that cared for the sick and dying sprang up among them to meet needs. As noted earlier, these associations came together in 1920 as the Order of Runeberg lodge. Picnics, sporting events, choirs, and lectures were sponsored. Newspapers were published and eagerly read.

As the flood of immigrants greatly declined after World War I, the second generation became primarily English-speaking. Finland-Swedish churches, like those of other languages (German, Norwegian, etc.), had to make the difficult switch to the English language. In 1961 the Baptist Mission Union went out of existence. Many of its members felt at home with the Baptist General Conference (BGC). Most of the Finland-Swedish pastors had been trained at Bethel Seminary when the majority of classes were taught in Swedish. Several descendants of this group have been important leaders in the BGC, including missionaries Eric Frykenberg, Ruth Bertell, Herb and Jean Skoglund, and Ken Gullman.

Dr. Emmett Johnson was a successful and much-loved pastor and district executive who led American Baptists in evangelism and became a vice president of the Baptist World Alliance. Dr. Clifford Anderson was a professor

Pastor Ted Johnson

My grandpa didn't want to serve under the Russian Army so he came to America to evade the Russian draft. He came here in 1879 (from Finland) and landed at the Statue of Liberty at Ellis Island. He came from what was Gamlakarleby at that time, which is Kokkola now.

My grandpa came here in 1879 because a couple of Grandma's brothers were here. Brother Matts had bought a half of a section—in fact that's where our farm was. Grandpa bought some from off of his brother-in-law Matts Newberg. And the other brother, John Newberg, had settled in Grand Rapids. He had . . . they were fruit growers . . . he had an apple orchard on the west side of Grand Rapids. There's a street there named Newberg yet.

My grandpa spent a winter of '79 with Uncle John, with his brother-in-law. And then in the spring he came up to Ensley Township of Newaygo County and got forty acres from his brother-in-law Matts. He worked, and he started raising sheep and built a log house. In fact, I was born in that log house. Of course the logs aren't showing any more. They're covered now. I was born in the house.

He raised sheep, and in the Old Country his trade was a dyer, to dye wool. But he knew the whole trade. So he would shear sheep, he would dye it, comb and card, and spin, and actually he made the clothes for his children for several years, even when they started going to school. In fact, they learned English by going to school. Swedish was spoken in the home. Now grandma came over a year later, after he got that house built in the summer of 1880. Later in the fall Grandma came over and joined him.

My father was a farmer, and he stayed on that same forty acres and added another forty acres to it. He was a farmer all his life, and they all spoke Swedish.

There was no Lutheran Church around there, and so a man by the name of Carmie Parker was at the grist mill when Grandpa took some grain to get ground at Ensley Center, and Carmie Parker asked Grandpa, "Do you go to church anywhere?" "No," he said. "I'm a Lutheran, and there's no Lutheran Church around here." Now really if there was a Lutheran Church he wouldn't have gone, to be honest. He was known as "Wild Peter" in the Old Country . . . "Peete Pilto." So, Carmie Parker said, "You see that log building down there about a third of a mile, that's the Free Methodist Church, that's where I go to church. Will you come there next Sunday and take your family with you and then come home with my family for dinner?" Well, that sounded good to this new Swedish immigrant, to be invited into an American home. And so that's what he did. And the spirit of God worked in his heart . . . and he turned to Grandma before the service was done and said that "we will be going to church here from now on." And he was marvelously converted. I tell people that the "Wild Peter" became the "Godly John." God has blessed his descendants. He had one son who was an ordained minister, four grandsons, and a step-grandson that are ministers, including me. Three great-grandsons that are or have been ministers . . . one of them is gone now. Going on to the fifth generation, we have a missionary. . . . Margaret Nelson, who is his great-great-granddaughter who has been a missionary all her life; to Taiwan, Hong Kong, and Phnom Penh, Cambodia. Another great-great-grandson who has been a missionary to Alaska. Two great-great-grandsons now are preparing for the ministry . . . but not all [are] in the Free Methodist Church. Some have gone to other denominations.

I was born and raised in the Free Methodist Church. I felt called into the ministry probably at the age of twelve or thirteen. I served in the military in World War II. . . . I was trained for the invasion of Japan. Hand-to-hand combat using the bayonet and butt of the rifle with the finger on the trigger. See, we figured we were going to have to invade Japan, and the old saying was that they would never surrender. And they wouldn't have if it wouldn't have been for the atom bomb. The invasion date was set for November 1. My group was set to come on November 2. We would establish a beachhead on November 1, and on November 2 my group would begin to move in and clear the land. So the atomic bomb probably spared my life. But I served there. I went to Spring Arbor Junior College at that time, and then I went to Hope College in Holland, Michigan, which is a college of the Dutch Reform Church. My wife was Dutch and she was from the Zealand area there, and her family was all Dutch background. But they happened to be Free Methodist too. I got my education there at Hope College, and I entered the ministry in 1952 in the Upper Peninsula. And that's where I met some Swedish Finns in the Marquette area. There's an area called Skandia up near Marquette, and that's heavy Sweden-Finn.

. . . Then I came down halfway to Traverse City and Petoskey for a few years. Then I was at Lansing for a couple of years, and Grand Ledge, and then I pastored here in Big Rapids for six years, in Grand Rapids for twelve years, and then for the last ten years of my ministry I was a conference superintendent. I traveled around and visited about forty different churches and gave oversight to them.

I retired in 1990, and in 1993 I became a principal of a little Christian school about twenty-two miles east of here. I held that for seven years until 2000, when my wife became so bad that I had to stay at home and take care of her.

I have no knowledge of them [Finland-Swedes]. I've lived here in Big Rapids—in fact, this is Swede Hill where I'm living—and at the foot of the hill by the river there is a big plaque that is dedicated to the Swede park, and there are twenty names or more . . . Swedish names, but I can't tell if they are Finnish or Swedish. At one time there was a Danish Lutheran Church, a Norwegian Lutheran Church, and Swedish Lutheran Church. They've all gone into one church now, Emanuel Lutheran Church. I've talked with them about it. They don't know of any Finns. If they were Finns they didn't identify themselves, and I'm just American now. My mother was American and my father, of course, Swedish. So, it depends if I'm with Swedes or Finns, I identify myself as such then, but otherwise I'm a blue-bellied Yankee.

Source: Interview with Retired Pastor Ted Johnson, Big Rapids, Michigan, March 5, 2010.

and later dean of Bethel Seminary San Diego. At least four moderators of the BGC were from the Finland-Swedish background, as was Dr. James Erickson, chair of the BGC Overseers for seven years. In the end, a small and faithful group of Finland-Swedes and their descendants have made a big impact within the Baptist General Conference.[143]

The first Covenant church organized by Finland-Swedes was in Brooklyn in 1900. The development of the church grew out of mission work started some years earlier. In Michigan there was a Covenant congregation in Ironwood, with others in Massachusetts and Connecticut. The activities of this church came to an end with the beginning of the Great Depression in 1930. To further the work of these churches, a monthly called *Svensk-Finska*

Third-generation Finland-Swede Clayton Carlson at his family farm in Cornell, Michigan. Photo by author.

Budbäraren was published in New York 1908–1925. During its best years the paper had about 800 subscribers.[144]

Around 1930 there were twenty Finland-Swedish Lutheran Churches, with about 4,000 members, and eighteen Baptist and Congregational churches, with 1,000 members between them.[145] Augustana Lutheran congregations remained dominant in the religious lives of Finland-Swedes. In the 1930s it was estimated that twice as many Finland-Swedish immigrants belonged to Augustana Lutheran congregations compared to their own separate Lutheran Churches. By the 1950s, most of the independent Finland-Swedish churches had either merged with Swedish-American congregations, had become completely Americanized through the influx of outsiders, or had ceased to exist.[146]

Some Finland-Swedes became involved with the Methodist Church as well. A small Finland-Swedish community developed in Cornell, Michigan, in 1904 and is best known as being home to the only Methodist congregation established among the Finland-Swedish immigrants in America. Meetings began in 1904 with visitations by Swedish Methodist Pastor C. H. Sundström from Escanaba.[147] While no Finland-Swedes are noted in the 1910 or 1920 U.S. Census, the 1930 census showed a total of twenty-two Finland-Swedes residing in Cornell Township, among them farmer Alex Carlson, whose family extends to the fifth generation and whose third-generation grandsons continue to maintain farms in the area.[148] In the early 1930s, the congregation was led by Rev. Karl J. Hammar, who pastored in Escanaba. The congregation in Cornell consisted of twelve to fifteen families, and a chapel church was built with cedar logs in 1934.[149] The congregation held Sunday school and confirmation classes, and a women's society was active for many years. In 1962 the congregation became part of the Central Methodist Church in the Escanaba parish, and membership included some of the descendants of early pioneer families and others who had moved to Cornell.[150] Eventually, the church was torn down, and today a residential building has taken its place. As noted by Rev. Scott Harmon, who is the current pastor of the Central Methodist Church in Escanaba, "There are literally no photos or records of the life of the [Cornell] congregation before 1931. Before Karl Hammer [sic], we know of only an immediate predecessor—a Rev. Paalm—through a single confirmation picture. No other histories or records exist save for a membership book (w/o pastors names). The Cornell church closed in 1972, with most of the members transferring to Central—the 'city' church. Descendants of those members from Cornell continue to be active in the church today. A handful remember, and were raised in, the log cabin church out there."[151]

Conclusions

Finland-Swedes are a small ethnolinguistic minority that deserves our attention. In Michigan many Swedish-speaking immigrants from Finland established their homes close to other Finnish immigrants, but some differences in distribution in the state exist. While Finns have remained dominant in Houghton and Keweenaw counties, Finland-Swedes have historically held more dominance in Dickinson and Delta counties. Concentrations in the Lower Peninsula, however, are not as well known or documented. A considerable concentration of Finland-Swedes was once found in areas such as Muskegon and Mason counties. Their work, community, and church activities were very similar to those of other groups. Some of the descendants of these early settlers still remain in the areas. Just as the residents of Brevort have rejuvenated their heritage and continue to celebrate the raising of the midsummer pole, it can only be hoped that similar interests will continue into the future. It is also hoped that much more will be uncovered in the future as scholars continue to search for insights and a better understanding of Michigan's ethnic populations. We are all richer for knowing and understanding the presence of our neighbors, all of whom ultimately have family roots elsewhere. We must celebrate this diversity and continue to preserve it. I hope this small insight helps us all.

Appendix 1

Finland-Swedish Recipes

Some of the best-known recipes that Finland-Swedes are associated with deal with the bounty of the sea. Various fish dishes are well known in Finland and were brought by immigrants to the New World. The following collection of recipes begins with the traditional Christmas entrée of lutefisk, which is shared by many Swedes and Norwegians as well.

Lutefisk: Fishy Rite Has an Air about It, by Karen Douglas

It wasn't the Christmas shopping that got me down last week. It was all the problems I had trying to locate all those little pink nose plugs to go along with Christmas Eve dinner. That's right, dear family. We're having lutefisk again. After all, the lye-soaked cod is *the* fish of a Scandinavian Christmas. Why, it's so popular that poems have been written about it, songs are sung, and Scandinavian sailors have been known to jump ship in the middle of the North Atlantic at the sound of its name!

Growing up with lutefisk as I did—with a Finnish-born mother and a Swedish father—I can only associate its pungent odor right along with the sweet fragrance of scented candles, pine greens—and Christmas. And, who am I, after all these centuries, to defy a family tradition because of a smell.

I must have been only five or six years old when I first remember Daddy   **73** coming home with that big white package tucked under his arm, which he promptly carried downstairs to the basement. It was just about two weeks before Christmas.

Following close behind, I stood by and watched as he carefully unwrapped the sun-dried cod, which strongly resembled a thick, white board— undoubtedly sturdy enough to sole your shoes. "What are you going to do with that thing?" I asked, with typical childlike curiosity. "Oh, just give the fish a little bath," he replied, filling the large galvanized steel tub with cold water. Day after day I watched as Daddy changed the bathwater, ridding the fish of the lye and making it fit for consumption. It wasn't long before the dry cardboard-type flesh began to swell and take shape.

By Christmas Eve Day, Daddy announced it was "ready." I watched again as he and Mama lifted the beautiful white fish from the bathtub, wrapped it in cheesecloth, and put it on the stove to cook in a large, white enamel pan. An hour later, the odor emanating from our kitchen defied description. "Oooooo! What's that awful, awful smell," I asked, as I watched my mother standing over the hot stove. "Hush, little one," my mother replied, in her broken English. "Go take your place at the table. Dinner's almost ready."

The dining room was bathed in the warm, soft glow of candlelight. Mama's best white linen cloth covered the festive table along with her best china, crystal, and the sterling silverware. Beside each plate was a small sauce dish filled with melted butter. Only on Christmas Eve would we have the special privilege of dipping our boiled potatoes in our very own sauce dish. "It's ready," Mama called from the kitchen. We turned and watched as she came through the door carrying the large platter, much like one of the three wise men bearing a treasured gift. The fish, covered with a nutmeg-sprinkled white cream sauce, was surrounded by parsley. As she set it down between Daddy and I, the white blob of jelly seemed to shimmer and shake. "Do we have to eat it?" I asked. "Oh, it's real good," Daddy replied. "Fish is brain food. Remember fish swim in schools," he said, with a wink of his eye—a characteristic I neither understood nor had accomplished at that age.

"Albert! Don't tell her that," my mother admonished as she placed a small portion on my plate. "Christmas wouldn't be Christmas without lutefisk." Seeing the frustration, and the obvious question written all over my face, my sister Anita came to my rescue. "Hold your nose, Karen, make sure it has lots of white sauce and cranberries on it, and get your glass of milk ready," she suggested, somewhat sympathetically. I took a bite. The small, slimy piece slithered down my throat. It didn't taste too bad—kind of like sea-flavored Jell-O. The thought was revolting.

Years later I learned Scandinavians often serve lots of strong spirits with this holiday delicacy. Scandinavians are smart people. Rice pudding—with an almond—followed the main course on Christmas Eve. To find the almond meant an extra gift. As I spooned my way through the creamy white pudding, I suddenly noticed that my fork had started to turn black. Now it was Sister's turn to ask a question. "Mom, if the lutefisk does this to the silver, what does it do to our stomachs?"

"Don't worry about it," Mama replied, ignoring the point of the question. "You and Karen can polish the silver tomorrow afternoon after we open our gifts."

Scandinavians are strange people. They sauna-tize their bodies and tarnish their stomachs. So it has come to pass that—for the sake of tradition—I made my annual trek to City Fish last week to purchase some lutefisk. It's now sold ready for cooking. "How much would you like, ma'am?" the clerk inquired. "One-half pound, please," I replied. "Uhhh, one-half pound? How many are you planning to serve?" he asked. "Four," I replied firmly. He looked as though he were about to say something, then changed his mind. He wrapped about a cup of the soft, white gelatinous substance in a small white package and handed it to me. I left the store.

How could I tell him that Christmas wouldn't be Christmas without that fragrant aroma of a much-cherished tradition? Besides, I don't want my daughters spending all Christmas Day afternoon polishing silver. They should easily have those four silver demitasse spoons clean in ten minutes.

O LUTEFISK (sung to the tune of "O Tannenbaum")
O Lutefisk . . . O Lutefisk . . . how fragrant your aroma
O Lutefisk . . . O Lutefisk . . . You put me in a coma.
You smell so strong . . . you look like glue
You taste just like an overshoe
But Lutefisk . . . come Tuesday
I think I'll eat you anyway

Source: Karen Douglas, "Lutefisk: Fishy Rite Has an Air about It," *Lansing State Journal*, December 18, 1985, 1C.

Jansson's Temptation

10 medium potatoes, peeled and sliced thin
10 anchovy fillets
1 onion, chopped
2-3 c. heavy cream

Layer in a well-greased casserole dish: potatoes, anchovies, and chopped onion. Pour half of the cream on top. Bake in moderate oven (375°F) for 1 hour. Add the remaining cream (or as much as needed to keep the potatoes moist). Continue baking until potatoes are well done. Serves 4.

Source: *Swedish-Finn Historical Society Quarterly* 2008, vol. 4, available at http://finlander.genealogia.fi/sfhswiki/index.php/Recipes_-_Quarterly_2008_vol4.

Fish Stock, by Anki and Gunnar Damström

1 gallon water
¼ c. butter
4 lbs. fish bones, heads, and trimmings
½ lb. yellow or Spanish onions
½ lb. leeks
½ lb. carrots
5 parsley sprigs
2 sprigs thyme

For fish bones select fresh halibut, rock cod, lingcod, or red snapper. (If in Finland, use abborre, flundra, girs, or hornsimpa.) Do not use salmon. Remove gills. Freshness of fish determines quality of fish stock. Rinse bones for 10 minutes under cold, running water.

Melt ¼ cup butter in a 2 gallon stock pot over medium heat. Gently simmer finely chopped onions for 10 minutes (do not brown onion). Add fish bones, trimmings, and water. Heat to a boil. Remove scum from surface. Add parsley and thyme sprigs.

Simmer for one hour. Strain fish stock through sieve. Return to pot and evaporate ¼-⅓ of the contents, leaving ¾-⅔ gallons in the pot. Pour stock into plastic containers. Let cool. Freeze. The fish stock lasts up to one year in the freezer.

For a delicious fish soup for two, heat two pints (½ liter) fish stock to boiling. Add finely cut chives, a can of corn, and 1 lb. (½ kg) of fresh fish filets cut into bite-sized pieces. Boil for two minutes. Enjoy.

Source: "Enjoying Old Family Recipes Q12-1," *Swedish-Finn Historical Society Quarterly*, available at http://finlander.genealogia.fi/sfhswiki/index.php/Enjoying_Old_Family_Recipes_Q12-1.

Hash (*Kött och Peruna*), by Dorothy Heslipen

Leftover roast, beef, or pork
Leftover or newly boiled potatoes
Leftover gravy
Leftover potato water

Monday was the day we had *kött o' peruna*. I guess you'd call it hash. The name we called it by is sort of hash too. *Kött* is Swedish for meat, and *peruna* is Finnish for potatoes. *O* is for *och* (and). That's what all the Swedish Finns called it. The meat was already done (from Sunday dinner) and the potatoes were cooked, so it was a matter of—well, Mother could cook the potatoes fresh if she wanted to, and then cube them—she didn't use onion. She'd cut the roast in cubes—not big cubes. She'd beat up the potato, add the meat, add the gravy. She knew after she'd stirred in the gravy how much liquid to add. She'd have some of the potato water in there too. I think that it was so good. It didn't take long to fix. It didn't take long to eat, either.

Source: *How We Cook Scandinavian: Recipes and Memories* (Ludington, Mich.: West Shore Scandinavian Society, 1993), 43–44.

Aunt Naomi Wilson's Rye Bread, by Dr. Margaret Gustafson

1 c. brown sugar
1 Tbs. salt
⅓ c. molasses
1 qt. milk
½ c. Crisco (scant)
4 c. rye flour

4 c. white flour

2 packages (5 tsp.) dry yeast

Mix sugar, salt, and molasses. Put Crisco in milk and scald. Pour over brown sugar mixture. Put 2 packages of yeast into ¼ cup of lukewarm water. (A little warmer for dry yeast). Add one sifter-full (about 4 cups) rye flour and mix into milk mixture. Let stand until almost cool. Put in yeast mixture and work it in again. Then add sifter-full of white flour (about 4 cups) and work in. Grease bowl all around. Put in dough, turning over so top is greasy. (This keeps the dough from drying out when rising.) Let rise until about double. Punch down and knead again. Divide into six loaves. Bake at 375°F for approximately 45 minutes. Makes six loaves.

Source: *How We Cook Scandinavian: Recipes and Memories* (Ludington, Mich.: West Shore Scandinavian Society, 1993), 38–39.

Åland Pancakes (*Ålandspannkaka*)

CREAM OF WHEAT:
4¼ c. milk
⅓ c. semolina
1 tsp. salt

4 eggs
7 Tbs. sugar
1 c. flour
1 Tbs. ground cardamom
2 tsp. vanilla sugar
(½ c. raisins)
3½ Tbs. melted butter
strawberry jam
(whipped cream)

A traditional specialty of the Swedish-speaking province of Åland Islands. Bring the milk to a boil and add the semolina and salt. Cook at a low heat for approximately 10 minutes while occasionally stirring. Set aside to cool. When cooled, pour the cream of wheat into a mixing bowl. Add the seasonings, sugar, eggs, (raisins), and flour and stir into a smooth batter. Cover a baking tray (with edges) with greaseproof paper. Brush the greaseproof paper with 3½ Tbs. of melted butter. Pour the batter onto the baking tray and cook at 400°F for 30–45 minutes, until golden brown. Serve the Åland Pancake warm together with strawberry jam, and whipped cream, if you wish.

Source: Converted from *Finnish Recipes and Foods*, available at http://www.finnguide.fi/finnishrecipes/recipe.asp?c=8&t=&p=126.

Coffee Bread (*Pulla*), by Dr. Margaret Gustafson

1 egg

1 tsp. salt

4 oz. butter or margarine

2 lbs. flour (approximately)

¾ c. sugar

1 Tbs. dry yeast

2 c. lukewarm water

1 tsp. ground cardamom (optional)

For glazing: egg

For decoration: chopped blanched almonds or sugar

Beat the egg and sugar. Add the lukewarm milk, the yeast (stirred in a coffee cup with the salt), and then sufficient flour to make a stiff, gruel-like mixture. This is worked until it becomes smooth and elastic, and only then is the rest of the flour added together with the butter—either melted or beaten to a foam. Knead the mixture into a pliable dough, cover with a baking cloth, and leave in a warm but not hot place to rise. When the dough has doubled in bulk, knead it on a table and shape it into small rounds or into long plaits made from ropes of even thickness. Lay these on a baking sheet and leave to rise again. Now brush the bread with egg and sprinkle either with the chopped almonds or sugar. Bake the long plaits for about 20 minutes in a moderate oven and the small rounds for about 7 minutes in a hot oven. When cooked, lift onto baking wire or table and leave to cool under a baking cloth.

Source: *How We Cook Scandinavian: Recipes and Memories* (Ludington, Mich.: West Shore Scandinavian Society, 1993), 39.

Runeberg Tarts (*Runebergintorttu*), by Beatrice Ojakangas

February 5 is the birthday of Finland's national poet, J. L. Runeberg. These
little cakes appear in bakeries in his honor.

DOUGH:

2 eggs
½ c. sugar
½ c. butter
1½ c. sifted flour
½ tsp. baking powder
½ cup ground almond

TOPPING:

1–2 Tbs. hot water
currant jelly
½ c. sifted confectioner's sugar

Cream butter and sugar together with an electric mixer until light and fluffy.
Add eggs and beat at high speed until creamy. Sift together the flour and
baking powder, and add gradually to the batter. Beat in the almonds. Butter
and sugar small muffin tins or tart pans (the authentic shape for these tarts
is a straight-sided cake pan about 2 inches in diameter and 2½ inches deep),
and fill about ⅔ full. Bake in a moderate oven (350°F) for 20 minutes, or until
pale golden-brown. When cool, dot each tart with about ½ teaspoon currant
jelly. Outline the jelly, using a force bag, with frosting made by mixing the
confectioner's sugar and water into a paste. Makes about 24 small tarts or 12
medium-sized tarts.

Source: Beatrice Ojakangas, *The Finnish Cookbook* (New York: Crown Publishers, 1964), 68.

Old-Fashioned Egg Coffee, by Karen Berg Douglas

8 c. water
6 Tbs. ground coffee
1 egg, slightly beaten
Dash of salt

Heat water in glass or porcelain-enamel coffee pot. Mix coffee grounds in small bowl with about 1 Tbsp of slightly beaten egg. (Cover remaining egg and refrigerate for use later.) When water begins to boil, add coffee ground mixture to boiling water and allow to boil for 2 to 3 minutes. Foam will appear on top of the pot. Remove coffee pot from heat and set on a cool burner. Sprinkle a few grains of salt into the pot and allow coffee to stand for 3 to 4 minutes, or until grounds settle to the bottom. Serve at once. Just be sure you don't shake the coffee pot when pouring it. (Some Scandinavians like to drink coffee the old-fashioned way by sipping it from a saucer with a lump of sugar between their teeth.)

Source: Karen Berg Douglas, *Coffee with Mama* (Lansing: Suomi-Sverige Publishing, 1994), 8.

Ida's Orange Fruit Cake, by Karen Berg Douglas

Ida (b. 1894) and Fred (b. 1895) Bostrom immigrated to the United States in 1914. The couple is known to have lived in Montana, where their son Francis was born in 1920. The family eventually moved to Michigan, where their daughter Margaret was born in 1922, and settled in Lansing. According to the 1930 census, Fred's brother Paul (b. 1906 in Finland) and a roomer, John Carlson (b. 1894 in the United States), also lived at the same Lansing address. Both Fred and Paul worked as machine operators at an auto factory. Ida Bostrom and my mother became best friends in 1928 when Mama emigrated from Finland to the United States. On February 2, 1994, Ida celebrated her 100th birthday. She was the matriarch of the local Scandinavian community and the only one to achieve a centennial anniversary.

1 orange
1 c. raisins
1 c. sugar
½ cup butter
2 eggs
2 c. flour
1 tsp. baking powder
⅔ c. sour milk
1 tsp. vanilla
½ c. nuts, chopped

GLAZE:

1 orange

½ c. powdered sugar

Remove rind from orange and place it and raisins through a grinder or food chopper. Set aside. In bowl, mix sugar and butter. Add eggs and beat well. Sift dry ingredients together and add to first mixture, alternately, with sour milk. Fold in orange-raisin mixture, vanilla, and nuts. Mix well. Pour into a well-greased tube pan. Bake for 1 hour at 350°F, or until a toothpick inserted into the cake comes out clean. When cake is cooled, glaze with juice of 1 orange that has been mixed with ½ cup powdered sugar. Pour or brush glaze over hot cake.

Sources: Karen Berg Douglas, *Coffee with Mama* (Lansing: Suomi-Sverige Publishing, 1994), 56–57, and 1930 U.S. Federal Census Record for Ida Bostrom, http:www.ancestry.com.

Famous Michigan Finland-Swedes

Every ethnic group can claim individuals who receive recognition and have achieved a status of respect among their peers, countrymen, and Americans at large. Finland-Swedes in Michigan are no different. Several noteworthy individuals are identified below, and it is hoped that while this is clearly not an exhaustive list, these few examples will attest to everyone's desire to succeed in a new homeland.

John Algot Markstrum of Dearborn, Michigan, was an engineer and inventor, born in Geta, Åland Islands, Finland, on December 4, 1889. He was the son of Andrew (b. 1847) and Amanda (b. 1852) Markstrum. Andrew Markstrum immigrated to the United States in 1891 and settled in Sherwood Township (today part of Clark Township) in Mackinac County, Michigan, where he took up farming. Wife Amanda and three children—Alfred, John, and Hannah—joined Andrew in 1899. To help supplement the family income in the early 1900s, John Algot crafted twelve violins as a teenager during the long winter months in northern Michigan. He excelled in school, earning a bachelor of science, master of engineering, and professional engineering degrees. He was a noted marksman, and legend has it that he was able to place a second shot in the same hole as his first shot from a distance of fifty yards. He became chief engineer with Continental Tool Works and was instrumental in the designing and tooling of the first American refrigerator in

1917. He designed car engines and was involved in building the Duesenberg racing engine that established the speed record of 1920. His inventions led to nine patents. He was the president and honorary member of the Swedish Engineers' Society of Detroit. He was also an accomplished author, writer, and lecturer. Markstrum also published the book *Les Cheneaux Pioneers* on Swedish immigrants to the Upper Peninsula of Michigan in 1973. He passed away July 4, 1980.

Finland-Swedish political figures are quite difficult to find. Some Finland-Swedish members in the Order of Runeberg in Vancouver have noted that former Michigan governor Jennifer Granholm is of Finland-Swedish ancestry; however, this rumor is based on the allegation that "there was a Granholm family from Finland who emigrated to Vancouver, B.C." Further research, and all published accounts of the Granholm family, clearly indicate that the family originates from Sweden.

One example of a less well-known political figure is Charles Evert Johnson, who served two terms as mayor of Ludington, Michigan, 1962–1966. He declined running for a third term, and it is possible that if he had run, he would have held the post even longer. Johnson was also instrumental in the development and founding of the West Shore Community College, which was opened to students in 1972.

Another Ludington resident was inventor Frank Johnson, who became a local celebrity due to his practical inventions that included a net lifter, an automatic temperature control for marine motors, a folding metal awning for windows, the first inboard/outboard drive for motorboats, an oil pump seal for mechanical pumps, and a door lock for refrigerators. Some of these inventions were later marketed and sold, and some were the forerunners of later refined inventions. Frank Johnson was born in 1891 in the 4th Ward of Ludington. His father, who was originally John Sunquist but changed his name to Johnson, was born in Finland. His life in Finland was easy, and he learned boatbuilding as well as farming. However, since the Russians controlled this part of Finland at the time, he, at nineteen, was subject to conscription in the Russian Army. He did what many of the European boys did during this period; he immigrated to the United States, where he knew no one and spoke no English. John came directly to Ludington and worked at times in the lumber industry, but most of the time he was a commercial fisherman. Frank, the oldest of nine children, and another brother worked on their father's boat for some years. John married Edla Borg in Ludington. When Frank was three, in 1894, the family moved to the Island, part of which was called Finn Town, and this is where the fisher folk lived. He lived there with the family until 1913, when they built a new house in Ludington. He was married October 1, 1919, to Clara Peterson, and they had one daughter, named Betty.

Johnson worked in commercial fishing with his own boat until 1939, when he decided that all signs pointed to the end of such fishing. In the years following, he sold boats, continued inventing, and worked on the 1914 breakwater and harbor, hauling and towing with his own tug. He also worked for a marine company on the Grand Rapids water pipeline from Lake Michigan. In Whitehall he was a production engineer with R. G. Company and the Austin Construction Company, building what later became the Dow Company. He also worked for Austin Engineering Company at Dow Chemical Company. He retired at age fifty-five and since then has been a freelance designer for some companies.

Material gathered from *They Made a Difference: Highlights of the Swedish Influence on Detroit and Michigan* (Detroit: Detroit-Swedish Council, 1976), 122; correspondence with Lloyd Markstrum, Santa Ana, Calif., October 11, 2010; and http://www.ancestry.com.

Correspondence with Syrene Forsman, Swedish-Finn Historical Society, Seattle, December 30, 2010.

Material on Charles Evert Johnson is difficult to find. The *Ludington Daily News* reported regularly on events involving City Hall, and Johnson was regularly noted in the press 1962-1966. Unfortunately, a detailed biography of the mayor was not available through sources such as the newspaper, Ludington City Hall, nor the White Pine Village Historical Society Archives.

Mason County Historical Society: Honorary Members—Biographies: Frank Johnson Family, White Pine Village, Mason County Historical Society, Ludington, Mich., no date on biographical material.

Notes

1. Reino Kero, *Migration from Finland to North America in the Years between the United States Civil War and the First World War* (Turku, Finland: Institute of Migration, 1974), 27.

2. Ibid., 34.

3. Ibid., 36.

4. Armas Holmio, *History of the Finns in Michigan*, trans. Ellen Ryynanen (Detroit: Wayne State University Press, 2001), 406.

5. Jouni Korkiasaari, *Suomalaiset Maailmalla* (Turku, Finland: Institute of Migration, 1989), 23–24.

6. Tom Sandlund, "Patterns and Reasons in the Emigration of Swedish Finns," in *Finnish Diaspora I*, ed. Michael Karni (Toronto: Multicultural History Society of Ontario, 1981). Carl Silversten believed that in 1930 "some 76,000 Swedish Finns [lived] in this country" (*Finlandssvenskarna i Amerika* [Duluth: Interstate Printing Company, 1931]). Holmio disputed this number as being an "exaggeration" (Holmio, *History of the Finns in Michigan,* 406).

7. Vern Mattson, *History of the Order of Runeberg* (Portland: International Order of Runeberg, 1977), 6.

8. Ancestry.com is the largest for-profit genealogy company in the world and runs a network of genealogy and family-related websites. For more information, see http://www.ancestry.com. HeritageQuest Online is a comprehensive treasury

of American genealogical sources—rich in unique primary sources, local and family histories, and aids for finding family members. For more information, see http://www.proquest.com/en-US/catalogs/databases/detail/heritagequest. shtml.

9. Steven Ruggles, J. Trent Alexander, Katie Genadek, Ronald Goeken, Matthew B. Schroeder, and Matthew Sobek, Integrated Public Use Microdata Series: Version 5.0 [Machine-readable database] (Minneapolis: University of Minnesota, 2010), http://usa.ipums.org/usa/.

10. Mika Roinila, "New Information on Finnish Americans," *AASSC Newsletter* (Association for the Advancement of Scandinavian Studies in Canada), no. 57 (November 2009): 7.

11. Hans Norman and Harald Runblom, *Transatlantic Connections: Nordic Migration to the New World after 1800* (Oslo: Norwegian University Press, 1988) and Eino Jutikkala, *A History of Finland* (New York: Praeger, 1962).

12. Correspondence with Dr. Margaret Gustafson, Ludington, Mich., February 11, 2010.

13. Helge Nelson, *The Swedes and Swedish Settlement in North America*, 2 Parts (Lund: University of Lund, 1943), Part I: 73, and Heikki Yli-Kangas, "Ostrobothnia in Finnish History," in *Finland: People-Nation-State*, ed. Max Engman and David Kirby (London: Hurst and Co., 1989), 73–84.

14. Mika Roinila, *Finland-Swedes in Canada: Migration, Settlement and Ethnic Relations* (Turku, Finland: Institute of Migration, 2000), 65, and Reino Kero, *Migration from Finland to North America in the Years between the United States Civil War and the First World War* (Turku, Finland: Institute of Migration, 1974), 63–65.

15. Kenneth McRae, "Finland: Marginal Case of Bicommunalism?" *Publius: The Journal of Federalism* 18 (Spring 1988): 91–100.

16. The Finland-Swedes of Ludington lived in Finn Town in the late 1800s and identified themselves as being Finnish, although they were clearly Finland-Swedes. Another example of this interethnic association was the attempt to start the Finnish Baptist Church in Chicago and the joint publication of *Finska Missionposten* in both languages. This effort failed and the Swedish language became dominant. The name of the church was changed to reflect this as well. For more, see Baptist Mission Union, "Bethel Baptist Church, Chicago, Illinois," in *Fifty Years of Christian Stewardship 1901–1951* (Baptist Mission Union of America, 1951), 31–33.

17. Roinila, *Finland-Swedes in Canada*, 74.

18. Elizabeth Oman, "Swede-Finns on the Iron Ranges of Northeastern Minnesota," *Finnish Americana* 7 (1986): 39–42.

19. Roinila, *Finland-Swedes in Canada*, 61–62.

20. Reino Kero, *Suureen Länteen: Siirtolaisuus Suomesta Pohjois-Amerikkaan* (Turku, Finland: Institute of Migration, 1996), 37.

21. Kero, *Migration from Finland to North America*, 16–17.

22. Ibid., 51; Korkiasaari, *Suomalaiset Maailmalla*, 27; and Roinila, *Finland-Swedes in Canada*, 64.

23. Anders Myhrman, "The Finland-Swedes and Their Cultural Organizations in America," *American Swedish Historical Society Yearbook 1957* (Philadelphia: Chancellor Press, 1964), 18.

24. Holmio, *History of the Finns in Michigan*, 406, and "The ASHM: A Museum for All Seasons," *American Swedish Historical Museum*, http://www.american-swedish.org/history.html.

25. Myhrman, "Finland-Swedes and Their Cultural Organizations in America," *American Swedish Historical Society Yearbook 1957* (Philadelphia: Chancellor Press, 1964), 18.

26. Ibid.

27. Ibid.

28. For information on the Research Data Centers, see http://www.census.gov/ces/.

29. Roinila, *Finland-Swedes in Canada*, 73.

30. Ibid., 80–85.

31. Randall was enumerated on August 3, 1850, and was recorded as a person who could not read or write. His identity as a Finnish-speaking or Swedish-speaking Finn is not possible. 1850 U.S. Federal Census Record, http://www.ancestry.com.

32. Holmio, *History of the Finns in Michigan*, 72–75.

33. John Wargelin, "The Finns in Michigan," *Michigan History Magazine* 24 (1940): 179–203, http://www.genealogia.fi/emi/art/article235e.htm.

34. Anders Myhrman, *Finlandssvenskar i America,* trans. June Pelo (Helsingfors: Svenska Litteratursalskappet i Finland, 1972), 202.

35. "1874—'God With Us'—1974 Emanuel Lutheran Church," centennial booklet, Ludington, Mich., 1974, p. 7.

36. Author-generated table obtained through IPUMS data at http://usa.ipums.org/usa/.

37. Myhrman, "Finland-Swedes," 18.

38. Wargelin, "The Finns in Michigan."

39. 1930 U.S. Census Records for Mason County. This number includes all individuals—adults as well as children of Finland-Swedish families. Data used elsewhere in this book only includes Finland-Swedes born in Finland with Swedish as their mother tongue. Descendants born in the United States are not included. Because of this, it is obvious that the total number of Finland-Swedes in the state in 1930 was well above the total of 2,525 established through detailed analysis. Data available at http://www.heritagequestonline.com.

40. Finland-Swedish settlement locations in Michigan are based on Myhrman, *Finlandssvenskar i America*, and Michigan Finland-Swedish communities as mapped by the Swedish-Finn Historical Society. See http://finlander.genealogia.fi/sfhswiki/index.php/Michigan.

41. Ibid.

42. Myhrman, *Finlandssvenskar i America*, 165-184. Available at http://finlander.genealogia.fi/sfhswiki/index.php/Northern_Michigan#cite_note-7.

43. Ibid.

44. Ibid.

45. "Gunnar Back," *Broadcast Pioneers of Philadelphia*, http://www.broadcastpioneers.com/back.html.

46. Myhrman, *Finlandssvenskar i America*, 165-184.

47. Ibid.

48. Ibid.

49. Interview with Clayton Carlson, Escanaba, Mich., July 27, 2010.

50. Ibid.

51. Interview with Richard Blixt, Escanaba, Mich., July 27, 2010.

52. Interview with Rev. Scott Harmon, Ellen Carlson, Nina Swanson, Nels Swanson, Rocky Blixt, Richard Blixt, Clayton Carlson, and Dory Carlson, Escanaba, Mich., July 27, 2010.

53. Myhrman, *Finlandssvenskar i America*, 179-181.

54. Roy Skog, "Erik Skog and Family," in *Felch Township Centennial Book, 1878-1978*, ed. Beatrice M. Blomquist (Norway, Mich.: Norway Current, 1978), 151-152. This book is a source for dozens of family histories, which is indicative of the presence of Finland-Swedes in the area.

55. Myhrman, *Finlandssvenskar i America*, 179-181.

56. Ibid.

57. "Felch Township, Michigan," *Wikipedia*, http://en.wikipedia.org/wiki/Felch_ Township,_Michigan. Although several attempts to contact Zion Lutheran Church failed in the summer and fall of 2010, it is hoped that future research will help uncover the current status of Finland-Swedes in the region.

58. Myhrman, *Finlandssvenskar i America*, 189.

59. Ibid., 190–192.

60. Holmio, *History of the Finns in Michigan*, 143.

61. 1930 U.S. Census Records for Gogebic County, http://www.heritagequestonline. com.

62. Ibid.

63. Interview with Leo W. Sved, Senter, Mich., April 1977, quoted in unpublished essay by William Sved, "Dollar Bay, Michigan: A Home for Swedish Speaking Immigrants," Department of Geography, Northern Michigan University, Marquette.

64. Roinila, *Finland-Swedes in Canada*; "Fishermen of the Keweenaw," *Finnish-American Reporter* (Hancock, Mich.), November 2002, 10–11.

65. Myhrman, *Finlandssvenskar i America*, 203–207.

66. As recorded in "Swedish-American: Michigan Churches," See Family Search at https://wiki.familysearch.org/en/Swedish_American:_Michigan_Churches.

67. Walter Romig, cited in Jeffrey Hancks, *Scandinavians in Michigan* (East Lansing: Michigan State University Press), 65.

68. 1910 U.S. Census Record for Oskar J. Eliasson, Houghton, Hancock Ward 4, District 120, http://www.ancestry.com.

69. Holmio, *History of the Finns in Michigan*, 107–109.

70. 1910 U.S. Census Records for Houghton, Hancock Ward 4, District 120, http:// www.ancestry. com.

71. 1930 U.S. Census Records for Houghton County, http://www.heritagequestonline.com.

72. John A. Markstrum, *Les Cheneaux Pioneers* (Hancock, Mich.: Book Concern, 1973), 76. It is interesting to note that Markstrum clearly identifies the residents of Mackinac County as Finland-Swedes, yet Brevort residents in the same county do not recognize the term.

73. Ibid., 22–23.

74. Correspondence with Lois Movalson, Brevort, Mich., November 22, 2010.

75. Walter Romig, *Michigan Place Names* (Detroit: Wayne State University Press, 1986), 76.

76. 1900 and 1910 U.S. Census Records for Mackinac County, http://www.heritage-questonline.com.

77. Excellent records of cemetery stones are available online that document the presence of Finland-Swedes in Western Brevort Cemetery, Moran Township, Mackinac County, Michigan. See cemetery photos taken June 22, 2003, available at http://www.genealogia.fi/haudat/index4e.htm.

78. 1930 U.S. Census Records for Mackinac County, http://www.heritagequeston-line.com.

79. Michigan Department of Conservation, Fishermen by Port: Licensed Commercial Fishermen 1966, Michigan Department of Natural Resources Records, courtesy of Thomas M. Goniea, Commercial Fishing Program, Fisheries Division, Lansing.

80. Correspondence with Lois Movalson, Brevort, Mich., November 22, 2010.

81. Correspondence with Pastor Jeremy Winter, Trinity Lutheran Church, Brevort, Mich., November 17, 2010. It appears that Romig, in his quotation about the roots of Brevort, as well as Pastor Winter both refer to the Finland-Swedes of Brevort simply as Swedes.

82. Finland-Swedish settlement locations are based on Myhrman, *Finlandssvens-kar i America*, and Michigan Finland-Swedish communities as mapped by the Swedish-Finn Historical Society. http://finlander.genealogia.fi/sfhswiki/index.php/Michigan.

83. Data available from http://www.ancestry.com.

84. Ibid.

85. Data available from http://www.ancestry.com.

86. G. Broända, "Eastern Bothnians in East Tawas, Michigan," in *Österbottningen*, trans. June Pelo Gamlakarleby (Finland, February 3, 1939), available at http://finlander.genealogia.fi/sfhswiki/index.php/Eastern_Bothnians_in_East_Tawas,_Michigan.

87. 1930 U.S. Census Records for Iosco County, http://www.heritagequestonline.com.

88. Myhrman, *Finlandssvenskar i America*, 151.

89. Ibid., 151.

90. 1930 U.S. Census Records for Kent County, http://www.heritagequestonline.com.

91. Interview with Carl and Margaret Newberg, Bethlehem Lutheran Church, Grand Rapids, Mich., July 7, 2010.

92. C. Evert Johnson, "Swede-Finns," in *Mason County Historical Society, Historic Mason County, Michigan 1980* (Dallas: Taylor Publishing Co., 1980), 88. The White Pine Village Historical Society Archives in Ludington provides several excellent sources, including some photos on the Finn Town of Ludington and an excellent map. See map 242, "The Island—Finn Town, 1890–1920," with detailed information on residence locations, names, and occupations, drawn by Frank Johnson, October 12, 1977. Other sources include Mary Sedlander's "They Called It Finn Town" (unpublished paper, Ann Arbor, Mich., 1990), and Dorothy Trebilcock's "Christmas in Finn Town around the Turn of the Century," *Ludington Daily News*, December 22, 1965. Also look for Mason County Historical Society Honorary Members—Biographies (Frank Johnson Family). Less well known is the fact that Charles Evert Johnson served as mayor of Ludington 1962–1966. He was also instrumental in the development and founding of the West Shore Community College, which was opened to students in 1972.

93. Although the mother tongue or language used by these immigrants is not noted in the 1870 U.S. Census for Newaygo County, it is very likely that these individuals were Finland-Swedes. The surname "Storm" is misspelled in the census as "Stoin." This census data was obtained through http://persi.heritagequestonline.com.

94. Myhrman, *Finlandssvenskar i America*.

95. Velma F. Matson, "White Cloud's Swedetown," *Quarterly* 18, no. 1 (2009): 1, 11–21.

96. Joelle Steele, *An Illustrated History of the Steele, Furu, and Forström Families in Finland and America* (Olympia, Wash.: Joelle Steele/Joelle Steele Enterprises, 2010), 121, http://swedishfinn.com/familyhistory-2010-col.pdf. Finland-Swedes arrived in Newaygo County at least as early as 1879.

97. Bror Åke Snickars, "Viktor from Uttermosta Built in the Swedish Town of White Cloud," *Vasabladet*, August 1993, translated in the *Quarterly* 11, no. 4 (1994): 81–82.

98. Matson, "White Cloud's Swedetown."

99. Deb Parrish, "Swedetown Today," *Quarterly* 18, no. 1 (2009): 1, 10.

100. Mattson, *History of the Order of Runeberg*, 10–11.

101. Anders Myhrman, *Memorabilia "Minnesskrift" of the International Order of Runeberg 1898–1968 in Words and Pictures* (Seattle: International Order of Runeberg, 1968), 5.

102. Mattson, *History of the Order of Runeberg*, 15.

103. Ibid., 13.

104. Myhrman, *Memorabilia*, 9.

105. John Berg, ed., *Minnesskrift 1902–1917* (Chicago: Svensk-Finska Nykterhetsför-
bundet av Amerika, 1917).

106. Myhrman, *Memorabilia*, 9.

107. The two publications include Thomas Stenius's *Svensk-Finska Nyterhets-För-
bundet af Amerika i Och Bild* (Chicago, 1908), and Berg's *Minnesskrift 1902–1917*.

108. Mattson, *History of the Order of Runeberg*, 24.

109. Ibid., 99.

110. Anders Myhrman, "The Finland-Swedes in America," *Swedish Pioneer Historical Quarterly* 31, no. 1 (1980): 16–33.

111. Ibid.

112. "Order of Runeberg, Dollar Bay, Michigan: History of Lodge 8," *International Order of Runeberg Historical Pictures*, http://www.orderofruneberg.
org/18historicalpictures.html.

113. "International Order of Runeberg List of Lodges 2010," *Leading Star/Ledstjär-
nan*, 104, no. 1, March 2010, 7.

114. Myhrman, "Finland-Swedes."

115. Emanuel Lutheran Church Register, Ludington, Mich.

116. This information is found at "Deward," http://www.ghosttowns.com/states/mi/
deward.html; "Manistee River Deward Tract," http://wolverineflyfishingjournal.
com/content/manistee-river-deward-tract; and "Our Great Uncle Adrian Oster-
lund in the 89th Division during the WWI," http://wordwithworks.wordpress.
com/2010/03/16/our-great-uncle-adrian-osterlund-in-the-89th-division-
during-the-wwi/.

117. Akseli Järnefelt, *Suomalaiset Amerikassa* (Helsinki: Otava, 1899).

118. Johannes Näse, "Finlandssvenskarna i Amerika," in *Svensk-Ostrobottniska Samfundet, Arkiv for Svenska Österbotten, Band 1, Häfte 3–4* (Vaasa, Finland: F. W.
Unggrens Boktryckeri, 1922), 245–275.

119. Myhrman, "Finland-Swedes."

120. Mika Roinila, "Finnish Commercial Fishing on the Great Lakes," lecture presented at FinnGrandFest 2010, Sault Ste. Marie, Ontario, July 28–August 1, 2010.

121. Lawrence Rakestraw, Commercial Fishing on Isle Royale: 1800–1967 (Houghton,
Mich.: Isle Royale Natural History Association, 1968), available at http://www.
nps.gov/history/history/online_books/isro/rakestraw/sec3.htm.

122. Evangelical Lutheran Church in America, "Augustana Synod," http://www.
elca.org/Who-We-Are/History/ELCA-Archives/ELCA-Family-Tree/Augustana-

Synod.aspx.

123. Evangelical Lutheran Church in America, http://en.wikipedia.org/wiki/Evangelical_Lutheran_Church_in_America.

124. According to Myhrman, *Finlandssvenskar i America*, the first two churches were established in Metropolitan and Thompson in 1895. However, I have found earlier congregations in the Lower Peninsula.

125. Bethlehem Lutheran Church, "About Bethlehem Lutheran Church," http://www.blc-grmi.org/about.htm.

126. Gary W. Morrison, "Church Marks 125 Years—Thanks to Its Families," *Grand Rapids Press*, 1999.

127. Interview with Carl Newberg, Bethlehem Lutheran Church, July 7, 2010, Grand Rapids, July 7, 2010.

128. Interview with Pastor Jay Schrimpf, Carl Newberg, and Margaret Newberg, Bethlehem Lutheran Church, Grand Rapids, July 7, 2010.

129. "1874—'God with Us'—1974 Emanuel Lutheran Church," 7-14.

130. Emanuel Lutheran Church Register, Ludington, Mich.

131. Emanuel Lutheran Church Transfers from Finland and Sweden (Book 1), Transfers from Sweden (Book 2-3), Ludington, Mich.

132. Interview with Pastor Jim Friesner, Emanuel Lutheran Church, Ludington, Mich., March 4, 2010.

133. Holmio, *History of the Finns in Michigan*, 407. The translation by Ryynanen incorrectly states that the "Lutheran church activity among Swedish Finns in Michigan is thought to have begun as early as 1805, when worship services for them were held in Metropolitan" (407). The village of Metropolitan was established in 1880 to exploit the iron ore in the nearby Metropolitan Mine. Metropolitan was about one mile west of Felch.

134. Sved, "Dollar Bay, Michigan," 23.

135. Holmio, *History of the Finns in Michigan*, 407.

136. Myhrman, "Finland-Swedes."

137. Baptist Mission Union, "Bethel Baptist Church, Chicago, Illinois," in *Fifty Years of Christian Stewardship 1901-1951* (prepared in commemoration of the fiftieth anniversary of the Baptist Mission Union of America, 1951), 31-33.

138. Ned Nordine, "Matts Esselström," *Cornerstone Baptist Church Pastor Biographies* (Ludington, Mich.: Cornerstone Baptist Church, 2010); Myhrman, "Finland-Swedes."

139. Myhrman, "Finland-Swedes."

140. Holmio, *History of the Finns in Michigan*, 408.

141. Baptist Mission Union, "Bethel Baptist Church, Chicago, Illinois."

142. "Swedish Finn Mission," *Ironwood News Record,* December 5, 1908, 2.

143. Clifford Anderson, Swede-Finns and the Baptist General Conference, Bethel University, St. Paul, Minn., 2002, http://www.bethel.edu/publications/trail-markers/past-issues/2002/october/index.

144. Myhrman, "Finland-Swedes."

145. Ibid.

146. Ibid.

147. Myhrman, *Finlandssvenskar i America*, 177–178.

148. See 1910, 1920, and 1930 U.S. Census Records for Cornell Township, Delta County, http://www.heritagequestonline.com. The 1910 census indicated several Finnish-speaking Russian Finns as residents of the township, but no Swedish-speaking Russian Finns. Material is also based on an interview with members of the Escanaba United Methodist Church, including Pastor Scott Harmon and C. Carlson on July 27, 2010.

149. Karl J. Hammar, *Saints, Sinners, and Hammars* (n.p, n.d.), 38–49. Most likely published in 1963 in conjunction with the retirement of Pastor Hammar, this book deals with the life and times of Pastor Hammar, who spent thirty-three years in the Escanaba-Cornell charge of the Central Northwest Conference of the Methodist Church. The text was provided courtesy of Pastor Scott Harmon, Escanaba, Michigan, by correspondence May 13, 2010.

150. Myhrman, *Finlandssvenskar i America,* 178.

151. Correspondence with Pastor Scott Harmon, Central Methodist Church, Escanaba, Mich., May 12, 2010.

For Further Reference

Archival Sources

Åbo Akademi Archives, Turku (Åbo), Finland. "The Myhrman Emigrant Archives." An excellent collection of materials dealing with oral histories, letters, articles, and photos from Finland-Swedes across the United States donated by Myhrman for the period 1900–1980. Several files deal specifically with Michigan Finland-Swedes, with the majority of this material written in Swedish. For more, visit http://www.abo.fi/public/en/arkiv_o_museer.

Finnish American Heritage Center and Historical Archive, Finlandia University, Hancock, Mich. The best source for Finnish American history in the country and the largest collection of Finnish-North American materials in the world, but unfortunately very little is available on Finland-Swedes. For more, visit http://www.finlandia.edu/fueled/fahc.html.

Institute of Migration Archives, Turku, Finland. The best source for archival material on Finnish emigration in the world, but disappointingly little on Finland-Swedes. Archives include letters, postcards, photos, photo slides, microfilm, audio recordings, interviews, and much more. For more, visit http://www.migrationinstitute.fi/sinst/archives.php.

Northern Michigan University Archives, Marquette, Mich. Some oral histories, articles, and photos on Finland-Swedes in Michigan are found in the archival holdings of NMU. Interviews conducted (on microcassette tapes) for this book are stored at the NMU Archives. For more, visit http://webb.nmu.edu/Archives/.

Swedish-Finn Historical Society Archives, Seattle, Wash. The best source for Finland-
Swedish material in North America. Historical materials about Finland-Swedish
emigration, books, artifacts, newspapers, articles, photos, and genealogical data
are available. Much is written in Swedish, but some in English and Finnish as
well. The SFHS is the official depository for the International Order of Runeberg
materials in the world. For more, visit http://finlander.genealogia.fi/sfhswiki/
index.php/Main_Page.

White Pine Village Historical Society Archives, Ludington, Mich. A good collection of
local history is available in the research library on Finland-Swedes who lived on
the "Island," along with some photos, articles, and a large detailed map showing
the Finland-Swedish settlement circa 1890-1920. Great source for further analysis of Finn Town. For more, visit http://www.historicwhitepinevillage.org/net/.

Further Readings

Alanen, Arnold R. "Finns and the Corporate Mining Environment of the Lake Superior Region." In *Finnish Diaspora II: United States*, edited by Michael G. Karni.
Toronto: Multicultural History Society of Ontario, 1981.

Blomquist, Beatrice M., ed. *Felch Township Centennial Book, 1878–1978*. Norway,
Mich.: Norway Current, 1978.

Hancks, Jeffrey W. *Scandinavians in Michigan*. East Lansing: Michigan State University Press, 2006.

Holmio, Armas K. E. *History of the Finns in Michigan*. Translated by Ellen M.
Ryynanen, edited by Philip P. Mason and Charles K. Hyde. Detroit: Wayne State
University Press, 2001.

Jalkanen, Ralph J., ed. *The Finns in North America*. East Lansing: Michigan State University Press, 1969.

Karni, Michael, ed. *The Finnish Experience in the Western Great Lakes Region: New
Perspectives*. Turku, Finland: Institute of Migration, 1975.

———. *Finns in North America: Proceedings of Finn Forum III*. Turku, Finland: Institute of Migration, 1988

Kaunonen, Gary. *Finns in Michigan*. East Lansing: Michigan State University Press,
2009.

Kero, Reino. *Migration from Finland to North America in the Years between the United*

States Civil War and the First World War. Turku, Finland: Turun Yliopisto, 1974.

Kolehmainen, John I. *The Finns in America: A Bibliographical Guide to Their History.*
Hancock, Mich.: Suomi College, 1947.

Markstrum, John A. *Les Cheneaux Pioneers.* Hancock, Mich.: Book Concern, 1973.

Myhrman, Anders. *Finlandssvenskar i America.* Helsingfors (Helsinki), Finland:
Svenska Litteratursalskappet i Finland, 1972.

————. *Memorabilia "Minnesskrift" of the International Order of Runeberg 1898–1968
in Words and Pictures.* Seattle, Wash.: International Order of Runeberg, 1968.

————. "The Finland-Swedes and Their Cultural Organizations in America." *American
Swedish Historical Society Yearbook 1957.* Philadelphia: Chancellor Press, 1957,
pp. 9–25.

Robbins, Paula Ivaska. *The Travels of Peter Kalm: Finnish-Swedish Naturalist, through
Colonial North America, 1748–1751.* Fleischmanns, N.Y.: Purple Mountain House,
2007.

Roinila, Mika. *Finland-Swedes in Canada: Migration, Settlement and Ethnic Relations.* Turku, Finland: Institute of Migration, 2000.

Index